The Advanced Placement Program in Italian: History and Analysis

Roberto Dolci

JOHN D. CALANDRA ITALIAN AMERICAN INSTITUTE
QUEENS COLLEGE, CITY UNIVERSITY OF NEW YORK

TRANSACTIONS
VOLUME 5

©2023 by Roberto Dolci
All rights reserved
Printed in the United States of America

John D. Calandra Italian American Institute
Queens College, CUNY
25 West 43rd Street, 17th floor
New York, NY 10036

ISBN 978-1-939323-20-0
Library of Congress Control Number: 2022951949

TABLE OF CONTENTS

vii   Acknowledgements

vii   Preface

1   Introduction

5   Chapter 1 — THE INITIAL YEARS
AP Historical Background — 5
The Scholastic Aptitude Test (SAT) — 5
The Birth of the Advanced Placement Program (APP) — 7
A Brief History of the Italian Language Certification in the USA — 9
The Regents Exam — 10
The Italian SAT — 10
The AATI High School Contest — 13
The AP Italian Language and Culture Program and Exam — 15
Conclusion and Further Research — 18

23   Chapter 2 — THE VOLUMES OF THE AP ITALIAN LANGUAGE AND CULTURE EXAM
Introduction — 23
Research Questions — 23
Method — 24
AP Exam Volume Exchange — 25
AP Foreign Languages Exams Volumes — 29
AP Italian Language and culture exam volumes — 30
The AP Exam during 2020 and 2021 — 33
Toward a Profile for the AP Italian Language and Culture Student — 39
Distribution of AP Italian Language and Culture Exam in the USA — 41
The AP Italian Courses Volumes — 44
The AP Italian Language and Culture Exam and Italian Ancestry — 49
The AP Italian Language and Culture Exam and Ethnicity — 52

57   Chapter 3 — ANALYSIS OF THE AP ITALIAN COURSE AND EXAM
Introduction — 57
The AP Italian program — 57
The AP Italian Course Description — 59
The AP Italian Language and Culture Exam — 64
The Structure of the AP Italian Language and Culture Exam — 65
The Analysis of the AP Italian Scores — 68
The AP Italian Scores Distribution — 72
The Free Response Questions Analysis — 77
The Chief Readers' Reports — 81
The Analysis of the Free Response Questions — 82
The Chief Readers' Recommendations — 87
Conclusions — 93

97   Bibliography

105   Index of Names

109   Author

for Barbara

ACKNOWLEDGMENTS

I had the opportunity to work with many of the people involved in the Advanced Placement Program (APP) in Italian,[1] especially in the critical phase of 2008-2012, from the announcement of the exam's suspension to its restart. I still vividly remember the commitment of several institutions, including Italian companies, various universities, the Italian Ambassador, students' parents, and teachers. They all felt involved not only as stakeholders, but also as ordinary citizens concerned about the fate of the Italian language and culture in the USA. I would thus like to thank all those who have allowed me to share this experience with them.

I had the distinct feeling that I was part of a team that had an important and unifying common goal. That experience gave birth to some "best practices" that are still employed today and that have also been replicated in other contexts, such as the Italian Language Observatory in the U.S. and the website www.usspeaksitalian.org, among many others.

It would be a pity not to continue to enhance such "expertise" and teamwork. Foreign Language teaching periodically undergoes moments of crisis. Only by sharing everyone's experiences and efforts, will we be able to deal with these inevitable moments in the future.

In the years that followed, I participated in organizing professional development courses for the AP Program in collaboration with or on behalf of various institutions, including the John D. Calandra Italian American Institute, the AATI, the Dante Alighieri Society, and the College Board. For the latter, I directed an AP Summer Institute at the University for Foreigners of Perugia in 2015. These experiences gave me even more opportunities to understand how precious and valuable Italian language teachers in U.S. schools are and how paramount it is to motivate, value, and encourage them.

There is so much more to be done in order to continue to effectively promote the Italian language and culture in the U.S.

I would like to thank Anthony Julian Tamburri, Dean of the John. D. Calandra Italian American Institute, who continues to host me as Visiting Scholar in Residence. He encouraged me to write this book; he then read, edited, and agreed to publish it. My gratitude also goes to all the members of the Calandra Institute for their support.

Many thanks also go to Maria Fusco, Dirigente Scolastica at the Embassy in Washington, who has provided me with valuable information; to Anthony Mollica, who read and commented on the first version of this study; to Michael Lettieri, former editor of *Italica*, for authorizing me to use an up-to-date and revised version of my essay first published in *Italica* 94.7 (2021); to Silvia De Paulis, who assisted with the English version and made many useful comments; and to Donna Chirico for her careful reading and suggested edits before going to press.

And, finally, to Barbara Spinelli, for her constant support.

NOTES

[1] College Board, Advanced Placement, AP, AP Central, and the acorn logo are registered trademarks of College Board.

Preface

Successful planning must start with the most detailed picture of reality. This axiom applies to all fields in which human intervention endeavors to change an existing situation. In order to put in place good planning and to prepare development strategies, it is necessary to understand fully the state of the art.

This is particularly true when dealing with complex systems, where there are many variables involved, often difficult to control, for example, in foreign language teaching. Each context has its own peculiarities, rules, and parties who interpret them and interact with each other and the environment in different ways.

In order to plan a valid educational policy, we must have exhaustive, valid, and reliable data. A careful analysis of this data will allow the administrators and stakeholders to optimize the often-scarce resources available, both human and financial.

Over the years, many studies have carried out quantitative and qualitative research on the study of Italian language and culture throughout the world; for example, Baldelli (1987), Freddi (1987), De Mauro, Vedovelli, Barni, and Miraglia (2002), Giovanardi and Trifone (2012), and Vedovelli (2011), which I shall reference in what follows.[1] Since 2014, the MAECI (Italian Ministry for Foreign Affairs and International Cooperation) has started an annual systematic collection of such data, which is easily accessible from its website devoted to Italian language and culture: *Italiana*.[2]

In the U.S., the initial research on the state of Italian language teaching dates back to almost one hundred years ago. The first survey with scientific intent was conducted in 1924. Its aim was to gather data on how many college students attended Italian classes.

The survey was carried out by Mario Cosenza, president of the ITA (Italian Teachers Association), the oldest association of Italian teachers in the U.S.[3] The investigation revealed a surprising vitality. 364 colleges recognized Italian credits for enrolment and 234 teachers delivered courses in the various colleges, with topics ranging from language to literature, from classics such as Dante, Petrarca, and Boccaccio to contemporary writers.

Cosenza explicitly stated that an adequate promotion strategy could be implemented only through a careful and periodic screening of the situation of Italian (Cordasco 1976). From 1924 to 1939, Cosenza produced a detailed annual report on the number of Italian language students in U.S. high schools and colleges. Cosenza's work is of inestimable value for having captured the situation of Italian in the period between the two World Wars. It was a pioneering and exciting period. Over the course of fifteen years, the teaching of the Italian language grew consistently. In high schools especially, it rose almost exponentially. This can be seen in Chart 1:

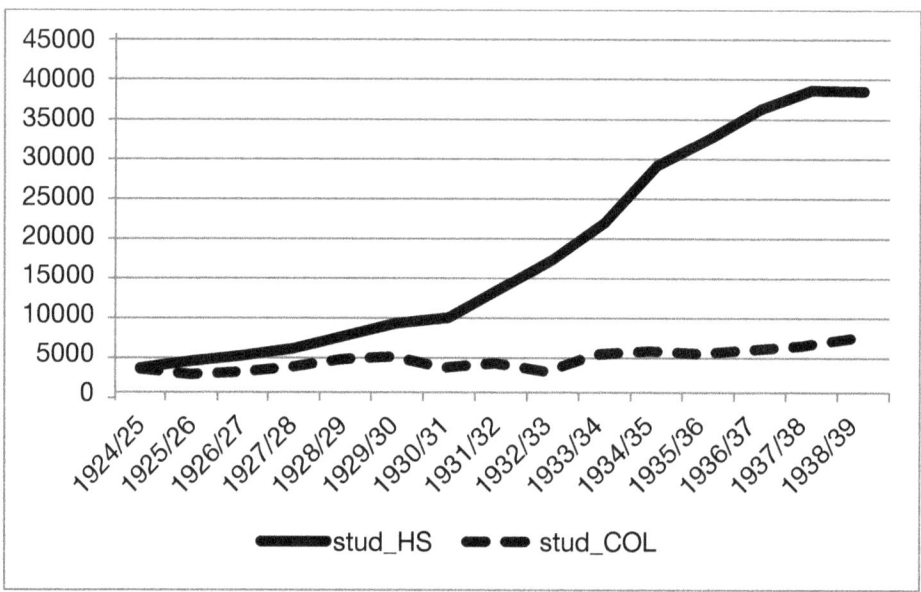

Chart 1: Students of Italian at HS and college from ITA Surveys (1924-1939)

Everyone was engaged in the enormous effort of promoting Italian; most notably the Italian/American community and the Italian government.[4] Teaching Italian was seen as an important tool for the Fascist regime to encourage the Italians abroad to support the regime's policy. For the Italian/American community, it was a tool to reaffirm its identity (Dolci 2018 and references cited therein). The first important success was the equal recognition with other foreign languages. This allowed the presence of the Italian language in increasingly more public schools, where, according to the last survey of 1939, students of Italian reached the figure of about 38,500.[5]

Cosenza's survey is only numerical and does not explain anything about who the Italian students were and what their motivation was to study it. All those involved in teaching and promoting the Italian language agreed that most of these students were of Italian origin, of second or third generation.[6] The efforts of both the Italian community at large and the Italian government specifically focused on avoiding the children of the immigrants losing their bond with their motherland, a bond kept alive by the knowledge of Italian. This aspect can be considered an element of strength because the community was very large. But it also represented a weak point, as it restricted the Italian language within the ethnic language borders, thus preventing it from expanding more widely. It is no coincidence that Mario Cosenza, in one of his reports, specifically mentions how he considers the enrolment of a single student of non-Italian origin more important than ten Italian Americans (Cordasco, 1975). This opinion was also shared by Giuseppe Prezzolini, in those years director of the Casa Italiana of Columbia University and at the forefront in promoting the Italian language in the U.S. (Dolci 2018).

The Second World War was a difficult time for the teaching of all foreign languages in the U.S., particularly for those of the enemy countries, accused of propaganda among young students. Mayor Fiorello La Guardia made a specific reference to this issue at the opening of the New York City school year in September 1940:

> Mayor La Guardia […] warned that foreign language teachers would not be permitted to introduce propaganda in their classroom work.
> *NY Times* (September 10, 1940): 1

Even though there were no official statistics, some scholars noted that for the years before and after the second World War, the Italian language lost about half of its students.[7]

For almost a decade and not until the end of the 50s, Italian was not included in the surveys carried out by both ACTFL (American Council of Teachers of Foreign Languages) in K-12 schools and the MLA (Modern Language Association) in colleges.

The MLA data on Italian students in colleges are considered the most homogeneous. These data were collected over a very long period of time and can therefore provide chronologically significant information.[8] Chart 2 shows the rate of college students from 1939 to 2016.[9]

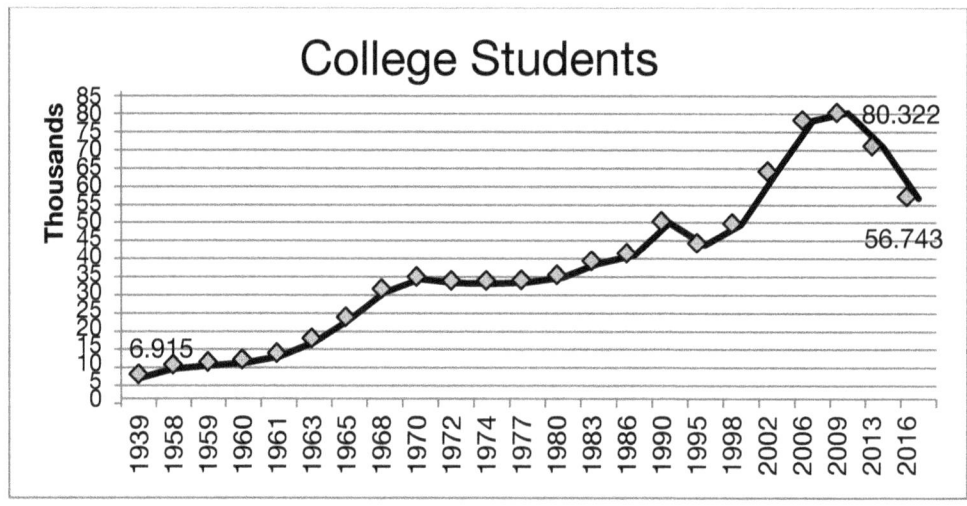

Chart 2. Italian Students at College (MLA survey)

Even if at a different pace, from 1939 to 2009, the growth appears to be steady. Whereas in the last seven years of the survey, there was a decline in Italian language enrolment in colleges.[10]

Chart 3 shows the number of students of Italian in public high schools from 1939 to 2000.[11]

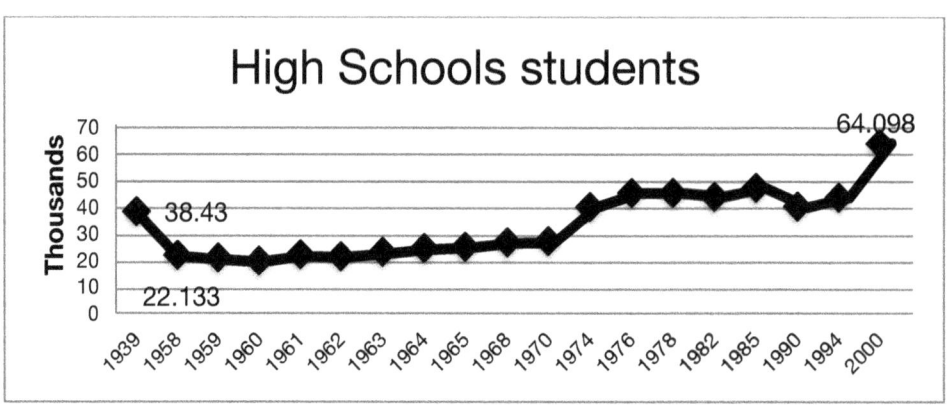

Chart 3: Students of Italian in Public High Schools in the USA

The drop caused by the Second World War was only recovered in the 1970s. Since then, there has been almost a constant growth, which was even more significant in the 1990-2000 decade. This ACTFL survey also shows that in 2000 there were 64,098 K-12 students in 37 states.

In later years, ACTFL also conducted two other surveys for foreign languages at K-12 level. In the 2004-2005 survey, the figure for Italian students is 65,058 in 14 states, while in the 2008 survey, the number of Italian students jumps to 78,273; 18 states replied to the questionnaire.

According to the latter survey, in 2008 Italian was in fifth place among the most studied languages at the K-12 level, after Spanish, French, German, and Latin.[12] Italian, however, would have had greater success if directly chosen by the students. As a matter of fact, a 2007 survey by the National Center for College and University Admission (NRCCUA), reported that students would have chosen Italian before other languages. The survey also indicated that this choice was made by about 50% of students of Latinx ethnicity. In 2008, a similar survey by ACTFL ranked Italian second after French.

The last survey on the status of foreign languages was conducted in 2016. The survey was sponsored by various U.S. agencies and associations, including the American Council for International Education (ACIE), ACTFL, the Center for Applied Linguistics (CAL), MLA, and the Defense Language and National Security Education Office. The survey included about 40 languages taught in K-12 schools in the U.S., varying from Spanish and French to Swahili and Lakota, from Chinese to Somali. Inexplicably, the teaching of Italian was left out.

Since 2014, the Italian Ministry for Foreign Affairs did however publish a series of quantitative data on the teaching of Italian in the USA. This data is organized into variables that do not always make them comparable with those of ACTFL or MLA. See Table 1.

	TOTALE STUDENTI	(a) studenti frequent. i corsi dei lettori di ruolo (1)	(b) globale studenti universitari	studenti scuole stat., parit., non parit. sez. bil./int. Sc.	(d) studenti scuole locali (2)	(e) iscritti ai corsi IIC	studenti corsi Enti Gestori	(g) studenti Società Dante Alighieri***	(h) studenti altri contesti
2014/15	212,528	676	71,699	345	44,205	3,401	74,664	4,193	14,021
2015/16	203,928	489	69,449	332	35,603	3,250	80,128	4,917	10,249
2016/17	221,741	601	73,479	298	46,475	3,636	86,109	1,784	9,960
2017/18	186.894	518	71.165	265	9,191	3,514	88,512	1,989	12,258

Table 1: Data for USA students. From MAECI surveys 2014-2017

This brief overview shows that the data collected from all these surveys cannot be considered reliable, since it was outdated and not comparable. These investigations have therefore provided a very blurred picture about the teaching of Italian in the U.S.

In order to develop an appropriate intervention strategy, we need valid and reliable data that can be comparable over time. A need to which the MAECI has committed to respond. Other local institutions, including the associations of teachers such as the AATI, also actively participate in resolving the issue.

In moving forward, I shall explore a peculiar aspect of the teaching of Italian in the United States; the Advanced Placement Program (APP), a small aspect but of great significance. Fortunately, there are detailed, valid, and reliable data, but there are no in-depth analyses yet. This book will attempt to offer one.

The history of the Italian AP is quite short, but the path that led to its realization is rather bumpy. All those who work or have worked for the success of the Italian language and culture in the U.S. — from the teaching, the organizing, and to the promoting of it — are well aware of this struggle. After 15 iterations of the exam, from 2006 to 2022, it is time to assess the situation. This book makes an initial evaluation of the results of the APP in Italian.

The first chapter deals with a historical reconstruction of the college access exams of Italian: the Achievement Test, the Scholastic Aptitude Test (SAT), the AATI National Italian Exam (NIE), and the APP in Italian. The second chapter and third chapters will analyze the AP Italian exams from 2012 to 2021.[13] The data are provided directly by the College Board, and the reports are prepared each year by the AP Chief Readers. The aim here is to provide some guidance for teachers, institutional bodies, and organizers. The conclusions will hopefully represent a contribution to the future of this important educational language policy tool, considered fundamental for the promotion of Italian language and culture in the U.S., and will represent a stimulus for researchers to deepen further analyses.

NOTES

[1] For studies on more specific contexts, see Vedovelli and Turchetta (2018) for Ontario, or Bettoni for Australia (1981, 1986) and Turchetta (2005).

[2] https://italiana.esteri.it/.

[3] Fucilla (1967), Cordasco (1975), and Dolci (2018).

[4] For my use of the slash (/) instead of the hyphen (-), see Tamburri (1991).

[5] Clearly it is underestimated, as it represented only the number of Italian students in public schools, thus, excluding many other realities, including the Dante Alighieri School courses.

[6] See Dolci (2018) and references cited therein.

[7] See Dolci (2018).

[8] There are also other surveys on the teaching of the Italian language in college. The most significant is the one conducted by Lèbano and Creech (1999) in 1983-1996.

[9] The source of 1939 data is ITA survey. It is used for indicative purposes only.

[10] This study will not dwell on the analysis of such data nor on the potential reasons for this trend. For such studies, it is preferable to refer to the analyses made by Angiolillo (1966), Striano and Adorno (1969), Haller (2016), Ryan (2016), and Cavatorta (2018).

[11] The figure for 1939 has been collected by the ITA survey, while the rest are the ACTFL data. Source ACTFL.

[12] In 2013 usspeaksitalian.org, built a database with schools and colleges that offered Italian language and culture. It showed that Italian was present in at least 30 states, plus the District of Columbia, with about 840 K-12 schools in total.

[13] The second Chapter is a revised and up-to-date version of an essay published in *Italica*, 97.4 2021.

Introduction

Over forty years, from 1880 to 1920, the population in America grew almost exponentially due to immigration. Consequently, the number of students attending schools and enrolling in college grew accordingly. The demand was so substantial that colleges sought solutions to regulate it. Some of them convened in order to develop standardized methods of selection.

The first methods were essentially based on achievement tests for specific subjects. In later stages, these tests evolved into the aptitude test, today known as the SAT (Lucas 2006, Liekar 2012, Jamison 2015, and references cited there).[1] Although considered a good starting point, this type of selection was also criticized for discriminating against certain ethnic groups (Hanson, 1992, 215).

Selecting the best candidates for college attendance, however, seemed insufficient. It also became necessary achieving a better connection between high schools and colleges in order to maintain continuity of the educational curriculum without useless repetitions (Fuess 1950; Barker, 1967).

This urgency explicitly emerged after the Second World War. Some reports showed that in many cases the introductory courses at the college level were practically a repetition of what the students had already studied in high school. (Fuess 1950; Liekar 2012; Jamison 2015). It was hence proposed to offer advanced courses in high schools. Students who would enroll in them and pass a final test would earn credits to bypass the introductory courses in college. The first Advanced Placement Course and its final test were officially offered in 1954 (Fuess 1950).

While there is a vast bibliography on the evolution of the SAT and the AP, information on the development and on the offering of Italian are incomplete. This information can be traced mostly through the reports of *Italica*, the AATI Journal.

Buchanan (1926) was the first to raise the issue of an Italian college admission achievement test. The offer of the Italian language SAT has continued to this day, even though with mixed fortunes and many interruptions. Alongside this test, which is prepared by an autonomous institution like the College Board, other exams have also been offered. In the sixties, the AATI started proposing a High School Contest which had the characteristics of the achievement test (Golden 1962). The exam is still offered today under the name of National Italian Exam (NIE). Instead, the AP Italian Language and Culture Course and the related exam were activated for the first time only in 2005-2006 (Mancini, 2006). The struggle of the institutional and professional bodies to achieve this goal has been long and hard, characterized by recent victories and failures.

As a matter of fact, in 2010, and only after four years, the AP Italian Language and Culture course and exam were suspended. Consequently, a considerable effort by the entire community was required in order to reinstate it in 2012.

Over the past few years, the Advanced Placement Program in Italian has been subjected to a "special supervision" by all the stakeholders who deal with the Italian language in the United States. All parties are aware that a further suspension could prove fatal for the very future of the AP Italian Language and Culture and thus have more general consequences. At the same time, the course and the exam represent a central asset in the language policy strategy of the Italian Embassy in the U.S. The Embassy constantly monitors its progress and continues to invest in it. The associations of Americans of Italian origin, the professional associations such as the AATI, teachers, students, and their families support the Embassy in this effort.[2] The entire history of the AP Italian Language and Culture Program is a clear example of how the objective of an educational language policy can be achieved. All stakeholders — indeed from different perspectives — join forces and coordinate themselves to achieve a common goal that can have positive, cascading effects for all involved.

Nevertheless, there are still no in-depth scientific studies on the Italian Language and Culture AP Program either at state or national level. There are not any specific investigations on the course itself, its aspects nor on the effectiveness of its promotion strategy. For example, there is no research on the methodologies adopted by the teachers, on the coordination between the syllabus and the exam, on the linguistic and methodological preparation of the teachers, or on their training needs. Unfortunately, there is no reliable information about the schools that offer it or about the reasons why other schools do not offer it either. No independent analysis has been conducted on the exam or on the results achieved by the students taking it. There are only the very useful and detailed data prepared by the

College Board itself. This contribution represents a first attempt at analysis. It is obvious that adequate strategies can be developed only with an accurate picture of the situation, done through the collection and interpretation of data from these resources as well. In this case, the goal is represented by the maintenance and development of the AP Italian course and its exam. The AP Italian Language and Culture Program is still "dangerously" close to the minimum survival threshold and must leave behind its precarious situation in order to secure a safe future.

The College Board data are in the public domain on its sites. My analysis will respond to these initial research questions:

1. What changed in the geographical distribution of schools offering the course and the exam?
2. How has the students' profile evolved?
3. Is there a progression of grades obtained in the exam and its different parts?

By analyzing the reports of the Chief Readers, this study will endeavor to show if and how these reports have been received by the teachers.

The main goal is for the entire scientific community to be aware of how important it is to conduct accurate and in-depth research on all the issues concerning the AP Program Italian Language and Culture. Such research is indispensable for an effective promotion strategy. In so doing, the AP can become an even more important driving force behind the growth of Italian language and culture courses both at K-12 level and in colleges.

NOTES

[1] Achievement test means a test that measures the skills acquired up to a certain time, while aptitude tests assess the ability of a person to reach a certain goal in the future. See Douglas Brown and Priyanvada (2004) for further reading.

[2] The essential instrument of this monitoring is the Italian Language Observatory in the U.S. A body that was established in order to coordinate intervention strategies both nationally and locally.

CHAPTER 1
THE INITIAL YEARS

AP ITALIAN HISTORICAL BACKGROUND

The College Entrance Examination Board (CEEB), or simply, College Board (CB), was founded at the end of 1899. It consisted of representatives of 12 colleges and three preparatory schools (Fuess, 1950). Its aim was to "design and administer standard entrance examinations that all member colleges would accept in making their admissions decisions" (Hanson, 1992). The reason why the CEEB was created is very clear:

> The College Entrance Examination Board was in its origin an attempt to introduce law and order into an educational anarchy which towards the close of the nineteenth century had become exasperating, indeed almost intolerable, to schoolmasters. The basic trouble lay in a lack of co-operation among colleges as a group and between colleges and secondary schools on the matter of college admissions. (Fuess, 1950, 3)

In fact, in the U.S. the transition from high school to college has always been an issue in the students' careers and for the smooth functioning of the entire educational system. Until the second half of the nineteenth century, each American college used different methods to select its prospective students.[1] But from 1890 to 1918, the high school student population grew by 711 percent. As a consequence, the number of students who wanted to enroll in a college grew exponentially (Hanson, 1992: 213, Romero da Silva 2017). The old selection system was no longer adequate.

THE SCHOLASTIC APTITUDE TEST (SAT)

The first test was administered in 1901. 973 candidates wrote essays in one of the following subjects: History, Greek, Latin, German, French, Mathematics, Chemistry, and Physics. These were achievement tests aimed at assessing the knowledge of specific subjects. These tests were suitable for managing and selecting a large number of students. Still, the assessment validity posed an issue. For this reason, an aptitude test was introduced in the 1920s. Its aim was to verify the general student ability to learn more than the knowledge of a specific subject.[2] It was considered a more effective tool for selecting suitable candidates for college.

The Student Army Training Corps as well, needed to effectively select candidates. This institution gave the opportunity to many recent immigrants enrolled in the army to access higher education even in universities that were previously considered very exclusive. Immigrants and veterans represented the most significant reason for the dramatic increase in requests for college enrollment. This raised strong concerns in part of academia since pseudo-scientific studies affirmed that certain ethnic groups were less intelligent than others.

> Early mental testers administered IQ tests to newly arrived immigrants at Ellis Island in New York City, which resulted in the exclusion of certain racial and ethnic groups. For example, in 1912 Henry Goddard "scientifically" proved that 90% of Hungarians, 87% of Russians, 83% of Jews and 79% of Italians were "feebleminded" (Cited in ETS Report, 1981: 42)

However, the first aptitude-type test developed by Thorndike in 1919 (Thorndike and Thorndike, 1920) proved to be more effective than the achievement tests. Therefore, CEEB commissioned psychologist Carl Campbell Brigham of Princeton to create one for the purpose of having an

> intellectual test ability without excessive reliance on any specific subject matter. This would promote the principle of equality of opportunity, in that discrimination against students from inferior secondary schools would be minimized. (Hanson 1992, 215)

The new test was administered for the first time in 1926 and since then has undergone several changes, both in name and structure, but it has always remained an aptitude test, which is now simply called the SAT.[3] Alongside the SAT, CEEB developed the SAT Subject Test or SAT II, offered for 20 different subjects, 12 of which are foreign languages, and Italian is one of them. The Educational Testing Service (ETS) has carried out all the examination tests proposed by the CEEB, since-its foundation in 1947.[4]

THE BIRTH OF THE ADVANCED PLACEMENT PROGRAM (APP)

The AP Program was created with the very specific purpose of inviting high schools and colleges to work together. It was specifically intended to improve students' training

- by facilitating the transition from high school to college;
- by avoiding repetition of course content;
- by stimulating the best students with more motivating programs (Lucas 2006, Liekar 2012, Jamison 2015, and references mentioned therein).

The period after the Second World War led to another significant change in the transition from high school to college. The outbreak of the Cold War and the subsequent war in Korea convinced the U.S. administration that an effective struggle against communism would also comprise greater attention to education. Engineers, scientists, and experts in other scientific disciplines were needed to fight and win this challenge. An important role was assigned to the knowledge of foreign languages (Flattau, 2006).

The launch of Sputnik in 1957 was a real shock. As the historian Daniel Boorstin (1973) said, "Never before had so small and so harmless an object created such consternation." Only well-trained teams of professionals could respond to such a technological challenge.[5] The entire U.S. educational path was then carefully examined to identify weaknesses and propose corrections. Once again, the transition from high school to college turned out to be a highly critical point. This time, however, for reasons different from those observed in the 1920s. In the 1920s experts criticized the excessive gap between high school and college, while in the 1950s they blamed the ineffectiveness of introductory courses in college (Liekar 2012).

To solve this problem, in 1951, the Ford Foundation launched the idea of allowing more prepared students to attend college courses before finishing high school. Superintendents and high-school principals strongly opposed this proposal. They would have lost their best students before their graduating year (Rothschild 1999, 176). The alternative solution was to allow outstanding high-school students to accelerate their educational path while in college.

In autumn 1951, a questionnaire addressed to former students at prestigious high schools such as Andover, Exeter, and Lawrenceville, to then seniors at Yale, Princeton, and Harvard, unveiled that, according to them, the college introductory courses were considered a waste of time.[6] The debate that followed led to a report named *General Education in School and College: A Committee Members of the Faculties of Andover, Exeter, Lawrenceville, Princeton and Yale*, published by Harvard University in 1952 (Rothschild 1999, 177) where the committee proposed to grant advanced placement to the best high school students (Liekar, 2012).[7]

In 1952, a commission of experts from various colleges was formed, and in May 1954 the first official Advanced Placement exam was administered by the Princeton ETS in 27 schools. The subjects offered were Biology, Chemistry, English Composition, French, German, Latin, Literature, Mathematics, Physics, and Spanish. The College Board took over the Advanced Placement program in 1955. Some of the rules established at that moment, such as the grades from 1 to 5, are still in place. Between 1955 and 1956, 1,229 students of 104 high schools took 2,199 exams, while 130 colleges and universities in the USA accepted Advanced Placement credits (Liekar 2012, 15).

Therefore, the AP Program was and continues to be the result of a shared effort between high schools and colleges, aimed at strengthening and improving cooperation between the two educational levels. Their target is to create a sort of "vertical curriculum" that optimizes the academic paths in order to eliminate unnecessary repetitions. It is a general belief that the Advanced Placement Program represents a positive stimulus not only for the students who take it, but also for teachers and schools who offer it. This tenet has been validated also by the research. Many studies suggest that students who attended AP courses and passed the final exam get better grades in college and graduate before those without an AP experience (Klaric and Morgan 2007; Mattern, Show, and Xiong 2009). Other researchers are more cautious (Pope 2013).[8] For example, some critics affirm that the AP favors privileged students, who come from schools with greater resources, and fosters certain ethnic groups in spite of others. It is true that some minorities are underrepresented in the AP, in comparison to the percentage of their presence in high schools.[9] In an interview,-for example, Pope stated that:

To the claim that they help students in college, it is true that students who take AP courses are more likely to succeed in college. But when you look deeper into the research, it's really hard to establish causation. It could just be that kids who take APs are kids who come from better high schools or high schools that better prepare them for college work, or they have better teachers or they're naturally more motivated. Very few studies use methods where they take these factors into account.[10]

Nevertheless, since 1955, the AP Program has grown steadily. Between 2018 and 2019, the College Board activated the AP Program on 38 subjects; 22,678 schools, 60 percent of the total, offered courses; 2,825,710 students took 5,098,815 exams, and 4,361 colleges granted AP credits (AP data, 2019).[11]

A Brief History of Italian Language Certification in the USA

It is not easy to outline the history of the Italian certifications proposed in the USA either as tools for admission to the college or, more generally, as tools to measure the student's achievement. Or, simply, in order to promote the study of the Italian language.

For example, it is not possible to find exhaustive references to the history of the Italian SAT in the official documents of the College Board or in independent studies. The only available documents that have allowed the reconstruction of the SAT history and the Italian Language and Culture AP Program are the ones included in *Italica* and in the *AATI Newsletter*. These documents have proved to be very useful sources in order to reconstruct the history of the teaching of the Italian language and culture in the USA. The reconstruction work will therefore be based on these two sources. Although these sources do not guarantee complete accuracy, the historical picture that will emerge is essentially authentic and significant.

The American Association of Teachers of Italian (AATI) is one of the oldest associations of Italian teachers and it has the highest number of members among school and college teachers. Since 1922, it has always had a pivotal role in defining the educational language policies that affect Italian in the U.S. and in Canada. Since 1924, the *Bulletin of the American Association of Teachers of Italian*, *Italica*, and the *AATI Newsletter* all reported on the initiatives and projects promoting Italian in North America. They also accounted for the struggles and subsequent requests for help in critical moments. Even if the information is sometimes fragmented, incomplete, and biased, through the reading of the minutes of their meetings, it is possible to get a picture of the teaching of Italian in North America over the last 100 years.

A quick reading of the debate between the promoters of Italian from American and Canadian institutions highlights how the comments were, at times, very harsh. Heated and passionate discussions also emerged for the certification: first for the SAT and subsequently for the AP. These discussions often led to both successes and failures. The spirit and motivation of everyone involved was, however, very high.

THE REGENTS EXAM

The first mention of an Italian language exam for high-school students appears in the *Fourth Annual Report of the Italian Teachers Association* (ITA) in 1924 (Cordasco 1975). From 1920, ITA was on the front lines fighting for the teaching of Italian in the New York area schools.[12]

In 1922, the New York City Board of Education stated that "Italian may be offered as an elective study, on an equal footing with other modern foreign languages" (ITA Report 1922, 28, cited in Cordasco 1975). In the same year, the first teaching certification in Italian for the New York area was offered.

Furthermore, in 1924 the Regents of the University of the State of New York offered the Regents test in Italian which was proposed, administered, and accredited for students "in precisely the same way and with as full credit as is attached to all other examinations conducted by the Regents themselves" (ITA Report 1924, 18, cited in Cordasco 1975).[13]

The head of the Italian Regents committee was Leonard Covello, who in those years played a decisive role in promoting Italian in New York. The Italian Regent was offered until 2011, when it was canceled due to a reduction in the State budget, following the fate of all other foreign languages Regent exams[14]

THE ITALIAN SAT

Any information regarding the existence of an Italian exam for college admissions is quite fragmentary and not easy to find. As I mentioned previously, the first SAT administered by the College Board (CEEB) was in 1901. Modern foreign languages included French and German. The first mention of Italian is found in the 1924 ITA Report:

> The [College Entrance Examination Board] has set examinations in Italian 2, 3 and 4 years in June 1924, and will do so likewise at the September examinations. This is the most widely known examining Board in the United States, and its setting examinations in Italian is a very important matter to those who have at heart the cause of Italian." (ITA Report 1924, 4, cited in Cordasco 1975).

A further reference is made in the following year's report: The Board "will continue to set, examinations in Italian 2, 3, and 4 years" (ITA Report 1925, 18, cited in Cordasco, 1975). At the time, Leonard Covello was appointed head of the committee for the implementation of the tests (ITA Report 1926, 33, cited in Cordasco, 1975). The test proved to be very successful. A year later the report revealed that 1,000 copies of each test for the first and second year of Italian had been distributed to New York City high schools (ITA Report 1927, 51, cited in Cordasco, 1975).

In 1950 The College Board subsequently announced that:

> The Achievement Tests used in the 1940's included Composition, Social Studies, Spatial Relations, Chemistry, Physics, Biology, and Reading Examinations in six languages: French, German, Spanish, Latin, Greek, and Italian. (Fuess 1950, 180).

From the citation, it can be inferred that from 1924 to 1940 the achievement test for Italian was regularly offered. Unfortunately, publications in *Italica* do not help in these first steps. *Italica* only mentions the presence of an achievement test in 1926, in one of its articles. The test was prepared not for the CEEB, but for the "American and Canadian Committees on Modern languages"; that is, the "Modern Language Association."[15] It is briefly described as still at the experimental stage.

The first mention of the College Board test for Italian dates back to the Editorial Comment in 1947. It was a rather laconic statement: "The College Board Examination in Italian will again be offered next in the same centers where this examination has been given in the past" (Fucilla 1947).

The second mention is more detailed. Castiglione (1959) argues that it would be necessary to encourage students to take the Italian exam offered by the College Board:

> We should bring about, in some measure, more conscientious teaching, as well as more serious preparation on the part of the student. (289)

Interestingly, the author emphasizes that the exam would encourage students as they would have a reason to better prepare themselves. It would also be good for teachers. The author goes on to stress the need for a standardization in the teaching of Italian, which did not yet exist. She also highlights an aspect that will be taken up often over the next few years: the program would become a reference point for teachers and their training.

In the early sixties, The National Defense Education Act (NDEA) funded numerous initiatives to promote Italian. As reported in the minutes of the *AATI Annual meetings*, the NDEA funded many initiatives devoted to the promotion of Italian language teaching such as Summer Institutes, scholarships for students and teachers, new textbooks, and the implementation of new tests for both students (Classroom Testing Program) and teachers (The Teacher Tests Certification) (Angiolillo 1967). The result was a remarkable increase in the number of students learning Italian (Golden 1962, 4; Falbo 1967). This rise had an impact on the number of students taking the CEEB SAT exam. The table in the *AATI Newsletter* published in *Italica* (3, 1966) (Angiolillo 1966), shows that it went from 141 students in 1960 to 637 for the Reading test and to 373 for the Listening Comprehension test, with a total of 1,010 students.

Unfortunately, this performance did not last. At the 1972 Annual Meeting, President Bruno Arcudi reported that the ETS canceled the examination test for Italian (Laggini 1973, 131). In response to the AATI protests, ETS replied that the blame should be on teachers, and therefore on the AATI itself:

> [Prof. Laggini] had been told in no uncertain terms that the teachers of Italian were to blame for the discontinuation of the test. It was the contention of the ETS that when the test was available very few orders

were received. When it no longer became economically feasible to print the tests, they were discontinued. (Laggini 1974, 103)

The College Board would also use the economic sustainability issue years later. The Achievement test was no longer discussed in the AATI *Annual Reports* until 1985 when AATI took the initiative to convince ETS to reinstate the test. The urgency was motivated by the belief that "the absence of such a test may be responsible for the lack of increased enrollment in Italian" (Mollica 1986, 430).

This action proved to be successful. In the 1987 Annual Report, after numerous requests, the president reported that ETS agreed to begin the procedure for the implementation of an Achievement test in Italian. The process would take about four years and the total cost would be around $350,000. The College Board funded the first year (Mollica 1988, 56). The test was reintroduced in June 1990 but did not achieve the expected results. The break-even point was fixed in 2,000 students (Kibler 1990, 106), but in 1992 only 900 took the exam (Kibler 1993, 295).[16] In that meeting, the possibility of offering an AP Italian Language and Culture Program was mentioned for the first time. But a sufficient number of students would be required to ew0create the Achievement test:

> It is hoped that the number [of the Achievement test] will increase more and that a listening component can be added. If there is an increase of 50% in the number of students taking the test, an advanced placement component can be offered. (1993, 295)

THE AATI HIGH SCHOOL CONTEST [17]

The certification promoted by AATI was first mentioned by Golden (1959). It was described as a "regular oral and written Italian contest examinations on the first-year and second-year levels to students in the secondary schools of the Greater Boston area." It was sponsored by the Eastern Massachusetts Association of Teachers of Italian (EMATI).[18] The initiative received attention from many other local chapters. Consequently, the following year a committee was set up to prepare a national contest on the model of the ones proposed for French and Spanish by their teachers' associations. It was 1960.

The project came at a bad moment for Italian. In an article published in 1962, Golden described a situation that was unquestionably not favorable for Italian. In high schools, it was the only language among the most important ones to lose ground; and even in colleges the situation was not encouraging. He writes that

> Italian can no longer be considered one of the most commonly taught languages in the United States. It might be necessary to include it on the list of critically needed languages unless new interest is shown in its study.

A few lines later, he writes in an ironic tone about the Italian National Contest: "Why should not the AATI have its national contest – just like the AATF and the AATSP?" (Golden 1962, 282; Falbo 1961, 1962, 1963).

The Italian Contest was "designed to measure competence in listening comprehension, speaking, reading, vocabulary, applied grammar, and civilization" (Golden 1960, 159). It was administered for the first time in the spring of 1961 (Golden 1964). From that moment on, it was offered every year until today.[19] In 1961, 1.132 took the two levels proposed. In 2009 it grew to 4,000 (Vitti-Alexander 2010).

I could not find detailed reports nor am I aware of specific analyses about the evolution and the status of the NIE. In the most recent *AATI Newsletters*, there are some statistical data that report a very positive situation. In 2017 the students were 5,465 from 184 schools (Bancheri 2017) while in 2018 they decreased to 5,418 students from 158 schools (Bancheri 2018). In March 2019, "5,353 students nationwide took the NIE, in particular we had 106 students at the Novice Level, 1,176 at Level 1, 1,262 at Level 2, 1,080 at Level 3, 656 at Level 4 and 167 at Level 5" (Maiellaro and Lubrano 2019).

Unfortunately, the data on the NIE found in the AATI's *Newsletters* are insufficient for any detailed analysis. These data would be very helpful to understand the NIE's success. Numerous factors are certainly involved and due to the following: there is effective and widespread promotion; also, NIE exam can be taken online. Perhaps, also, because, being a contest, it distributes prizes, medals, small sums of money, and scholarships to the best students, whose names are then published every year in the *AATI Newsletter*.

The AP Italian Language and Culture Program and Exam

After the first notation in 1993 (1, 295), *Italica* reports on the AP Italian Language and Culture Program again only in 1999. In the *AATI Newsletter Spring* 1999, AATI President Kleinhenz emphasizes the importance of an "AP-Like" test for Italian and announces the appointment of an *ad hoc* committee in collaboration with the American Association for Italian Studies (AAIS) (Kleinhenz 1999; Epstein 1999).[20] Kleinhenz underlines that this type of exam will help students to continue their study of Italian in college, and above all, to proceed after the initial levels. As the first course of action, the *AATI Newsletter* proposes a questionnaire of interest for both high school teachers and college professors. In the introduction, the authors say that "[t]he elaboration of the exam and relevant course(s) should foster more exchange of information and greater collaboration between high school and academic colleagues" (Kleinheinz 1999, 8).[21] In the meantime, a new opportunity emerged: a collaboration with the College Board for an official AP Program. This collaboration was supported by Italian institutions. The AATI representatives decided to collaborate with the Consulate General of Italy in New York and prepared a proposal to the College Board (CB). If the College Board would reject the proposal, AATI and AAIS would implement their "AP-like" exam (Giordano 2000, 143). The idea was welcomed by many teachers and by associations representing the Italian/American community. The proposal was presented to the College Board in January 2001. The prospects seemed very good. The College Board required that at least 500 schools declare their intent to participate in the program. In fact, the high schools where Italian was taught at that moment were around 800: all of them could have been responsive (Pagano 2002, 140).

But hopes clashed with a harsh reality. A College Board survey carried out in 2001 showed that only 167 schools were interested. Too few to think about starting the program. In addition, the College Board required a $500,000 co-financing to develop the program. The community was not discouraged. On the contrary! It launched various initiatives to find other schools and to obtain financing (Mita 2002). All the members of the community, from institutions to parents, did their utmost to achieve this goal. After a more detailed investigation, 493 schools declared their interest in starting an Italian AP Program. In the meanwhile, the Italian Government and the major Italian/American associations guaranteed the co-financing. As Mita points out, the College Board itself was impressed by the community's cohesion and organization. As a result, in June 2003 it approved the development of the Italian AP Program (Pagano 2004, 134; Sclafani, 2004, 134). The following two years were devoted to developing the syllabus and the exam, to training teachers, and to promoting the AP Program throughout the Nation (Nuessel, 2004).

The Advanced Placement Italian Language and Culture test was administered for the first time on 8 May 2006. 1,597 students took it. Unfortunately, there was not much time to celebrate this important result. Already in January 2008, the College Board expressed its concerns about the continuation of the Italian AP Program (Tamburri 2009, 3). The College Board pointed out to the community representatives that the numbers they reported to start the program were actually highly overestimated. Instead of 493 schools, as they had declared, in 2006 only 311 high schools activated the APP. In 2007 they dropped to 305. Similarly, students who took the exam in 2007 increased by "only" 3 percent reaching the figure of 1,642. Far too few, according to the College Board, to make the Program financially self-contained (Tamburri 2009, 3). The College Board insisted that "it was expected that there would be approximately 500 schools and 10,000 students involved in the exam" (Tamburri 2008, 2). The reality was too far from expectations. Despite all the efforts to avoid it, on January 6, 2009 the College Board announced that the Advanced Placement Program in Italian would be suspended after May 2009 (Tamburri 2009).

There are several reasons for this failure, even though the most important is the economic one. It definitely was not due to the scarce interest in the study of Italian. In fact, as reported above, 4,000 students enrolled in the High School Contest in 2009. A noteworthy achievement. Also, on closer inspection, considering the four editions of the AP Italian Language and Culture exam from 2006 to 2009, a significant growth is noted: if in 2006 the students were 1,597, in 2009 they were 2,282, an increase of about 40 percent. The schools' enrolment went from 311 in 2006 to 422 in 2009. Therefore, the number approached the threshold of 500 schools required by the College Board.[22]

Based on these data it can be said that the College Board decision was probably too hasty. After all, the promotional strategies implemented at that time by the community proved to be successful. Perhaps only a little more time and more pressure on the College Board were necessary.[23]

From this brief and incomplete summary, it can be easily understood why the community learned, with deep concern, the news that the AP Italian would be suspended. The concern was accompanied by a sense of frustration and impotence when, in the *AATI Fall 2009 Newsletter*, the President, Anthony Julian Tamburri, wrote:

> The AP in Italian remains in some sort of limbo, to put it nicely, held hostage by a series of circumstantial vagueries no one seems to be able, or willing, to unravel.

But there was still hope: "Suspended. Not cancelled!" (Lanza 2009 p. 6). The frustration did not last. Aware of what was at stake, the community once again lined up to restart the Italian AP Program.[24]

The reinstatement of the AP Italian Language and Culture Program was a "major academic and cultural issue. [...] A basic, bare bones issue" (Tamburri 2008). It was linked, in certain ways, to the very survival of the teaching of Italian in the USA. At the same time, the struggle also assumed other aspects. It stressed the importance of an identity pride for the Italian, Italian/American and the more general italophile community in the USA.

The contribution of the Italian language and culture to Western civilization was emphasized, as it always happens in such cases. Finally, it represented another episode of the fight against any possible discrimination for the teaching of Italian with respect to languages "that have more currency, we've been told, within the greater United States collective consciousness." (Tamburri 2009a; Tamburri 2009b). The contribution of Italian culture to the Western world and the discrimination against Italians are two recurrent aspects in the campaign for the promotion of Italian language in the USA and, more in general, into the debate about the diasporic phenomenon (Dolci 2018; Butler 2001).

This "call to arms" still had the effect of strengthening the community in achieving a shared goal central to its identity. This time the College Board set $ 3,000,000 as the required amount to restart the AP Italian Language and Culture Program and increased the number of exams to 2,500 as the threshold to be reached by 2016.

Once again, the amount was equally divided between the Italian government and the associations of Americans of Italian origin, with the essential contribution of some Italian companies and a significant share of donations from individuals.

The AP Italian Language and Culture Program restarted in the sacademic year 2011-2012: 1,806 students took the exam on 17 May 2012.[25] The figure of 2,500 was reached in 2015, one year earlier than expected, with 2,573 students. The session in 2019 saw the participation of 2,658 students, after touching the peak of 2,926 students the year before. In 2020 and 2021, due to the COVID-19 pandemic, AP Italian language and Culture exam numbers show a decrease, like all the AP exams in other subjects, Foreign Language included. In 2020 2,518 students (a drop of 5 percent) took the AP Italian exam, while in 2021 2,102 (a drop of 17 percent) took, while in 2022 2.194 students took the exam. Although we are still dangerously close to the threshold, we can say that AP Italian Language and Culture Program is planting its roots. The effort now is to consolidate this growth and continue to grow.

CONCLUSION AND FURTHER RESEARCH

An approximate calculation shows more than 8,000 Italian exams taken by middle- and high-school students each year in a combination of the NIE, the SAT II or the AP Italian language and Culture Exam. This number certainly indicates success, but it still raises questions. Is it the result of an accurate and coordinated strategy or the random result of a series of single interventions? Is it possible to improve on it? How?

One might ask, for example, if there is a relationship between the various exams, tests, and contests proposed for Italian, the NIE, and the AP in the first place. For example,

- Are students taking both the NIE and the AP?
- How many are they?
- The exams are held a short distance from each other. The NIE is in March, the AP in May. Could this represent an issue?
- Do the students know what the difference is between NIE, SAT II, and AP?
- Do colleges accept NIE scores as they do AP scores?
- Finally, is it possible that the exams are in competition?

These are only a few questions of concern. There are many others. In the Fall 2019 *AATI Newsletter,* Beppe Cavatorta, then president of AATI, writes the following about the AP:

> La minima flessione nel numero di studenti che hanno sostenuto l'esame AP di lingua e cultura italiana non deve suonare come un campanello d'allarme ma ci ricorda che non siamo nella posizione (*e forse non lo saremo mai*) di poter abbassare la guardia. (Cavatorta 2019, 1)[26]

Regarding the NIE, the AATI rightly states that it is proud of its success. In 2019, Maiellaro and Lubrano write the following:

> The NIE Committee envisions the exam not only as an assessment tool, which provides teachers and students with diagnostic feedback and positive wash-back to help inform high school instruction and curricula, but also as an opportunity for visibility and for promoting Italian programs in North American schools.… (Maiellaro and Lubrano 2019, 11)

In its website, the AATI expressly "encourages instructors of Italian to invite their students to participate in the National Italian Exam, which could help them prepare for the official exams of *Seal of Biliteracy*, the SAT II and finally, will make them eligible for the *Società Onoraria Italica* scholarships."[27]

The AATI's campaign to promote the NIE seems to be very incisive and intense. Surely, it has been successful, given the results.[28] However, one could ask if, more generally, this is the best strategy. If the exams also serve to promote the teaching of Italian, would it be better to concentrate the efforts on a single exam or to distribute them in a different way along the students' career? For example, is the option to offer the NIE only to middle schools and in the early years of high school, leaving grade 11 and 12 at the APP, a viable one? Why, and how many, 11th and 12th grade students decide to take the NIE instead of the AP exam? Do teachers recommend choosing between them? What are the differences between the two exams for credit recognition?

It is important to collect data to answer these and similar questions. It is crucial that all the institutions draw up an effective and coordinated language policy strategy for the promotion of Italian that also includes the exams offered for Italian. This is another very important research project for the future of Italian in the U.S.

NOTES

[1] For example, some assessed the student's competence in specific subjects: mainly the classical ones such as Latin and Greek. Literature and history, and the more scientific ones such as mathematics and geography would gradually be added (Barker, 1967, 250). Furthermore, the selection method was different among the colleges. Some went directly to the high schools to select the best students, others did rehearsals on campus, etc. (Hanson, 1992: 213).

[2] Intelligence tests had emerged as an assessing tool during the First World War in order to select soldiers and distribute military tasks and duties in the best possible manner. The best known is the Thorndike Tests for Mental Alertness (Hanson 1992, 214; Barker 1967, 251).

[3] The current SAT has four sections: Reading, Writing and Language, Math (no calculator), and Math (calculator allowed). See the official SAT web site at the College Board. https://collegereadiness.collegeboard.org/sat.

[4] An in-depth description of the SAT and its evolution is not the purpose of this work. See ERS Report (1981), Stewart and Johanek (1996), Lawrence, Rigol, Van Essen, and Jackson (2003).

[5] The National Defense Education Act (NDEA) was the most important and response given by the administration to this challenge. It gave a significant boost not only to the teaching of sciences, but also to foreign language teaching including Italian (See also Bigelow and Lyman (1964) and Flattau (2006) and the references cited therein). Between 1960 and 1970 *Italica* reports many projects financed with NDEA funds aiming to spread Italian language teaching and learning. Such as Italian courses, teacher training courses, travel scholarships in Italy, etc.

[6] "The college work was too easy. So, I drank, and wasted time, and ran down to New York. I didn't have to work so I didn't. […] I am seriously convinced that I was magnificently prepared at school and my first three terms at college were a total loss" (cited in Rothschild 1999, 175).

[7] As Rothschild points out the report, "given the elite character of the institutions involved," was 'unashamedly elitist throughout'. (1999, 177)

[8] The research conducted by Klaric & Morgan (2007) and Mattern, Shaw and Xiong (2009) have been commissioned by the College Board. See also Pope (2013) who analyzes more than 20 studies on the AP Program.

[9] The *New York Times* demonstrated interest in this theme. See the article written by Maria Newman (and published on February 9, 2011).

[10] "Are AP courses worth the effort? An interview with Stanford education expert Denise Pope." *Stanford News*, April 22, 2013. https://news.stanford.edu/2013/04/22/advanced-placement-courses-032213/ retrieved October 2019.

[11] In 2020 and 2021 data are a bit different. Probably due to the COVID-19 pandemic, in 2020 students were -6,5 percent with respect to 2019 and in 2021 -3,6 percent with respect to 2020. The number of exams decrease consequently. The number of schools offering AP exams in 2020 was -2,3 percent with respect to 2019, but in 2021 it registered a +2,9 percent with respect to 2020.

[12] It has also played an important role at the national level. The annual survey conceived by its president, Mario Cosenza, was until 1939, the most accurate source of information on the state of the teaching of Italian in the USA. See Dolci (2018).

[13] The Regent exam is prepared by the New York State Board of Regents and administered to High school students in grades 9-12 or at the end of high school. https://www.schools.nyc.gov/school-life/learning/testing/ny-state-high-school-regents-exams. Retrieved October 2019.

[14] In 2018-2019 the New York State Education Department has approved the Italian Checkpoint B Examination (Oneida-Herkimer-Madison BOCES) and the Italian Comprehensive Exam (*New York City Department of Education*) as Department-Approved Pathway Assessments in World Languages.

http://www.nysed.gov/curriculum-instruction/ world-languages-approved-assessments. Retrieved January 2022.

[15] Buchanan (1926). In the *Modern Language Journal* there are few references to the CEEB test during the years 1920-1940. An article published in 1928 is dedicated to it (Brinsmade 1928). It is cited mainly in articles concerning French, about ten articles, German (1919, IV, 1) and Spanish (1928, XII, 4). No reference to the Italian test was found. For an overview of the research on testing in the MLJ, see Spolsky (2000).

[16] In 2019, 1287 students took the Italian SAT. (https://collegereadiness.collegeboard.org).

[17] Later named "AATI High School Contest"; then "National Italian Contest." Today it is the "National Italian Exam."

[18] EMATI would become the AATI New England Chapter in that year.

[19] The exam changed many times. From 2016 on it is offered online (Petrarca Boyle 2016). The NIE is now aligned with the *ACTFL Performance Descriptors* and the *2012 ACTFL Proficiency Guidelines*. From 1971 AATI offers also the College Essay Contest (Laggini,1971).

[20] Many people are involved in the history and the chronicle of the AP exam, from the ambassador to many experts, entrepreneurs, presidents of associations, up to those who are on the front line: teachers, students, and their parents.

[21] The quality and quantity of relationships between high school teachers and college teachers have always been, and continues to be, hotly debated topics among AATI members.

[22] From the documents consulted, it is not clear on what basis the College Board indicated the number of 10,000 students and if this was the figure that would guarantee the economic sustainability of the AP Italian. In any case, it was clear from the beginning that it would have been practically impossible to reach it in a short time, as the AATI president A. J. Tamburri himself pointed out in his message (Tamburri 2008, 1).

[23] The doubt was currently being raised. See the President's message (Tamburri 2009, 1)

[24] The hypotheses of replacing the AP with a test created by the AATI was excluded. Official certifications for Italian issued by Italian universities were also rejected. Decisive was the discussion during and after a fundamentally strategic conference on the promotion of Italian in the USA organized by the Embassy of Italy in Washington in June 2009, "Conference on the Promotion of Italian Language in U.S. Schools K-16 and Continuing Education Washington D.C. - June 13, 2009" The conference brought together Italian and American experts, jointly with representatives of the Italian Government and the Italian/American community. The feasibility of an online Italian AP exam was also evaluated. This option was excluded at least for the time being (Vitti 2010)

[25] The 2010 and 2011 interruptions caused the loss of more than 10 percent of students. Another uphill start; and further proof of how the College Board's decision to suspend the program in 2009 was, in hindsight, too hasty.

[26] Translation: The slightest drop in the number of students taking the AP Italian language and culture exam should not sound like a wake-up call but remind us that we are not in the position (and perhaps never will be) to be able to let our guard down.

[27] https://aati.uark.edu/aati-national-exam/ (visited November 2019). We are not aware of any studies that have verified the achievement of these objectives. The precedent version of the page, visited in 2018, said that the NIE would prepare also for the AP exam.

[28] Also, The National Association of Secondary School Principals has placed the NIE on the NASSP National Advisory List of Contests and Activities for 2022-2023.

Chapter 2
The Volumes of the AP Italian Language and Culture Exam

Introduction

Based on the situation described in chapter one, it is necessary to try to understand if, where, and how to intervene to guarantee for the AP Italian Language and Culture Program a constant growth that helps to move away from the logic of emergency and survival. This chapter will provide an initial answer to some research questions related to this goal: it represents the first attempt at an analysis of the AP Italian Language and Culture on the part of the scholarly community. It makes no claim to being exhaustive; it is simply intended to represent the starting point for what must be an ongoing tracking of the AP Italian Language and Culture Program. Such monitoring should produce not only scientific analysis, but also data useful for better planning language policy interventions, promotion, teacher training, etc.

Research Questions

Consider the following questions:

- Is the Italian AP distributed evenly among U.S. states or is it concentrated in a few areas? The question is related to the obvious hypothesis that if it expands in more regions, it has greater opportunities of increasing the number of schools and students that can assure its survival.
- Has the percentage of students who scored 1 to 5 changed over the years? The answer to this question can provide insight into the link between the Course and the Exam, and into the urgency of specific teachers' professional development.
- Is Italian learned basically by heritage learners, those with Italian ancestry? Or has it also expanded to other ethnic groups? Who are they? Is it worth investing in them?

Unfortunately, as we shall see, some of the answers to these questions will remain incomplete and thus unreliable due to the lack of data available for many aspects of Italian language teaching in the U.S. It is a problem that needs urgent solutions.

METHOD

The College Board provides professors, administrators, and the scientific community with an accurate statistical analysis of the AP exam. This praiseworthy activity guarantees first and foremost the transparency of the College Board's work and the quality and validity of the process. Moreover, it represents a very useful tool to understand the status of the program and of every single subject. The data allow both cross-sectional and longitudinal analyses, up to a time span of more than 20 years. Every year general and subject-specific information is processed. Data regarding the number of exams, students, schools, and colleges that accept the AP grades are distributed. The distribution of scores and their variation over time are provided. The analysis also includes the students' ethnic groups. The data are distributed at national and state level, including Canada.[1]

From 2006 to 2022, the AP Italian Language and Culture exam was subjected to several disruptions: it was suspended in 2010, again in 2011, and the course description went through a major change, starting in 2019. Also, in 2020, due to the COVID-19 pandemic, the structure of all the AP exams had been completely changed. In order to maintain reliability, data will be analyzed accordingly to these events.

The College Board also makes available a series of specific data on the AP Italian exam. For example, each task of section II, the Free Response Questions (FRQ) section, is analyzed separately. These data serve as the basis for the report that the Chief Reader draws up each year. In it the Chief Reader: compiles feedback from members of the reading leadership to describe how students performed on the FRQs, summarize typical student errors, and address specific concepts and content with which students have struggled the most that year.

While this report is mainly addressed to teachers, it is also extremely useful for administrators and for all other people who are concerned with and work on the AP and the promotion of Italian language in the U.S.

The second part of this analysis, in turn, identifies the strengths and weaknesses of each task and the students' performance; it also analyzes diachronically the recommendations proposed by the Chief Readers, aiming at identifying, if possible, whether and how their advice has affected the work of the teachers.

AP EXAM VOLUME EXCHANGE

In what follows, I will present the numbers of the AP Italian Language and Culture Exam and analyze its trend, both over the long term, from 1955 to 2022, and over a shorter period. In so doing, let's keep in mind the pandemic's very notable impact on AP examinations in 2020 and 2021. Thus, an analysis of the trend in the figures regarding exams, students, and schools can only be done with the understanding that the 2020 and 2021 data were heavily influenced by the pandemic and thus cannot always be used to describe the trend over the medium to long term. In addition, in 2020 the examination was held in a completely different mode than the standard mode. I will also need to keep in mind that two Course and Exam Descriptions are in effect in the 2011-2022 period. The first one from 2011 to 2019, the second one from 2020 onward.

I will first briefly present the general data, concerning all disciplines, then focus on that of foreign languages, comparing the data of Italian with the languages that can be considered "competitors." Finally, I will analyze separately the data that interest us most closely, those on AP Italian Language and Culture.

In Chapter 1 I reported that the first AP Course was offered in 1955, with the first exam session offered in 1956. Since then, it showed a constant increase both in the number of schools and in the number of exams taken until 2019. In 2020 and 2021 data show a decrease, while in 2022 the numbers of schools, students, and exams increase once more.[2]

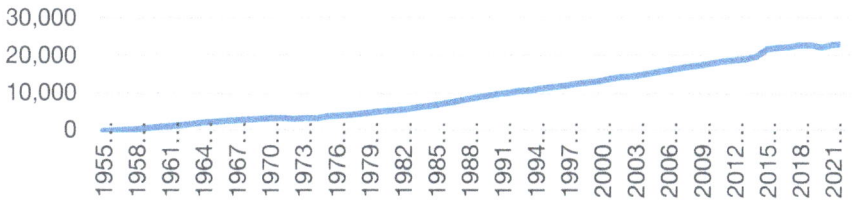

Chart 4: Number of schools offering the AP Exam

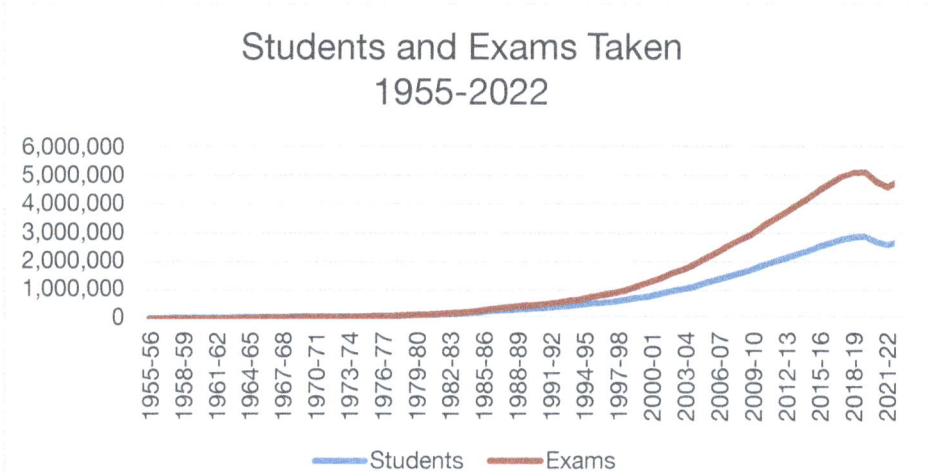

Chart 5: Number of exams and of students who took them. The numbers differ because each student can take more than one exam.

Chart 4 and Chart 5 clearly show the steady growth of the AP exam over its nearly 70 years of existence, in terms of the number of schools involved, the number of students and, consequently, the number of exams. Note in this respect how, from the late 1980s onward, the spread between the number of exams and the number of students is widening further and further: it is increasingly common for a student to take multiple AP-level courses and consequently take multiple AP exams of different subjects. The figure is a testament to the success of the AP Program among students and families who see the AP Program as a good investment in the student's career when he or she goes to college.

Numbers reached their pick in the session of 2019, when 22,678 schools offered the AP exam, while 2,825,710 students took 5,098,815 exams in 38 different subjects. 4,930,147 exams in the USA, 31,927 in Canada, 136,741 in other countries around the world. In 2020, there were 2,642,630 students taking the exam, a decrease of about 6.5 percent from the previous year. In 2021, students who took an AP exam were 2,548,228, -3.57 percent compared to 2020. So, from 2019 to 2021 the decrease was about 9.8 percent. Similarly, the number of exams taken decreased from 5,098,815 in 2019 to 4,578,308 in 2021: a reduction of 10.2 percent. Since 2022, the numbers are going up again: the number of exams taken was 4,762,347 (+4 percent over 2021), and the number of students taking an AP exam was 2,659,914 (+4.3 percent over 2021). A significant increase, but it is still far from the 2019 figures.[3]

Let's look at chart No. 6 where the trend of all subjects from 2012 to 2022 is presented. It is a narrower period, but still revealing. Although the chart is not easy to read at first glance, we can still draw some observations. First, there is a big difference between the subjects. The volumes go from more than 500,000 exams for English Language and Composition to just over 2,000 for Italian Language and Culture and Japanese Language and Culture. Also, some have a more regular trend, such as Music, French, European History. Others show very fast growth, such as Seminar, Research, and Computer Sciences Principles. Others are experiencing greater fluctuations than other disciplines, such as Human Geography and Psychology.

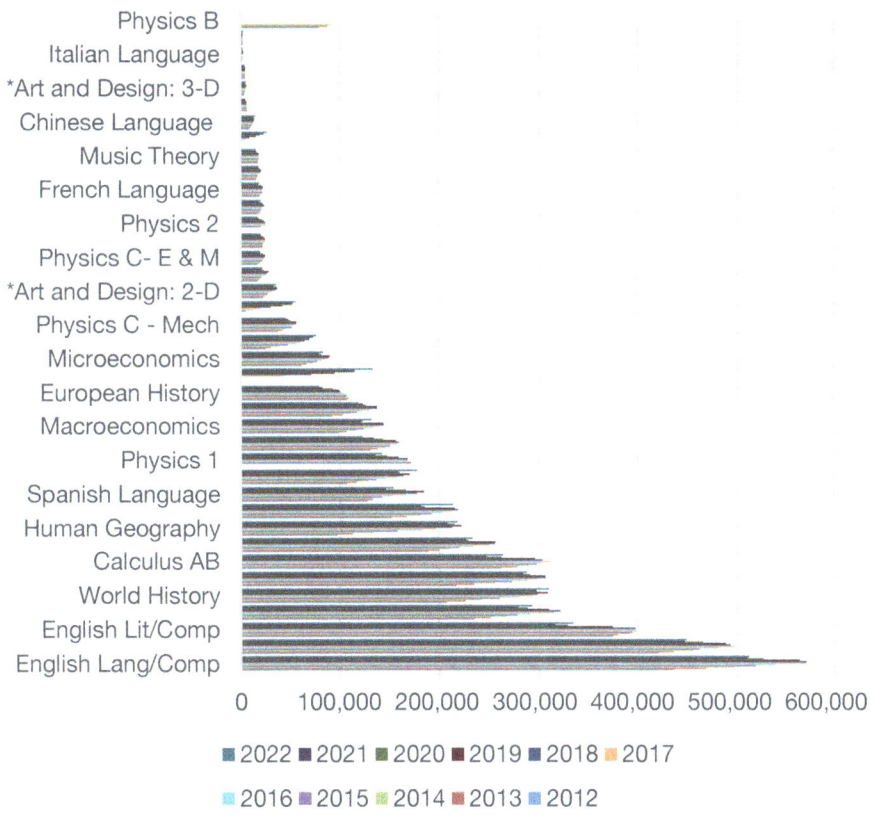

Chart 6. AP exams in all subjects. 2012-2022

Between 2012-2022 the five most popular subjects are always English Language and Composition, U.S. History, English Literature and Composition, U.S. Government and Politics, and World History. They consistently have the highest numbers and by themselves and cover about 40 percent of the total AP exams. See the graph below.

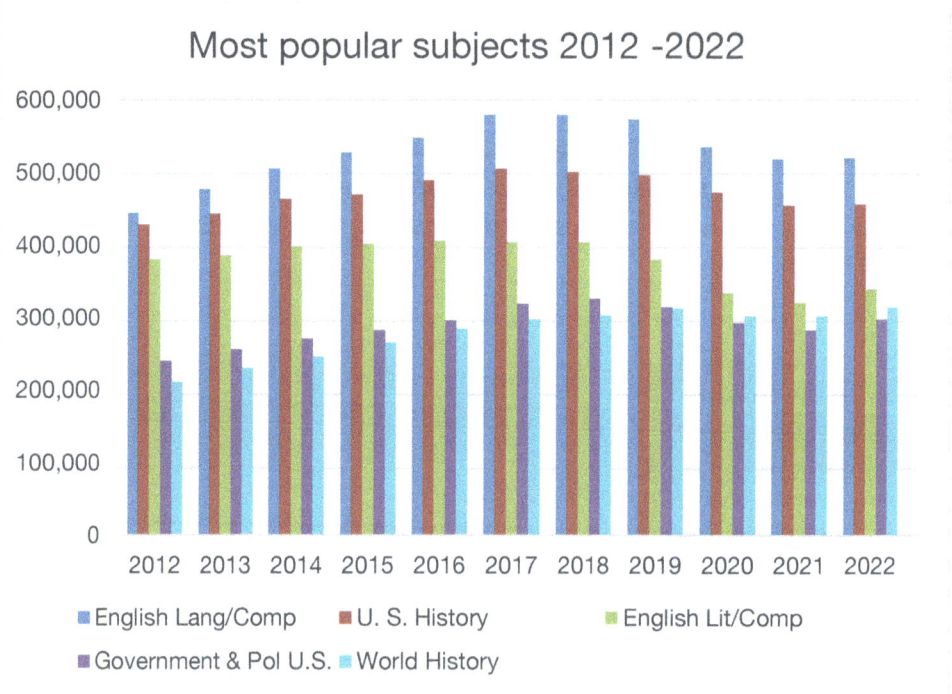

Chart 7: The five most popular subject for the AP exam 2012-2021

All the five subjects are over 300,000 exams taken. English Language and Composition normally surpasses 500,000 exams, followed closely by U.S. History, which reaches 496,573 exams in 2019. Further behind, English Literature and Composition, 380,136 exams, U.S. Government and Politics 314,825, and World History, 311,215 exams in 2019. They are closely followed by Psychology, Calculus AB, the top science subject, with 300,659 exams in 2019, and three other subjects above 200,000 exams: Biology, Human Geography, and Statistics. These ten subjects, out of a total of 38, account on average for more than 60 percent of the total number of exams.[4]

AP Foreign Languages Exams Volumes

Let us now look at an area closer to our interests. The College Board offers an AP Program for seven foreign languages: Chinese, French, Italian, Japanese, Latin, Spanish, and German. Spanish is the only language that offers two AP programs, one for language, the other for literature: Spanish Language and Culture and Spanish Literature and Culture.[5]

Based on exam numbers, we can divide the languages into three different groups; on the one hand, Spanish, then, French and Chinese, and then the remaining languages: German, Latin, Italian, and Japanese.

In 2019 the total number of AP exams in foreign languages accounted for about 5 percent of the total exams taken. But the numbers for Spanish cannot be compared to those of the other foreign languages, due to the special status of Heritage Language that Spanish has in the U.S. In fact, in 2019 Spanish Language and Culture reached 187,133 exams and exceeded 200,000 if we include Spanish Literature and Culture (29,345 exams in 2019); about four times the total of all other foreign languages. From 2012 to 2022, Spanish constantly occupies eleventh place among the more popular subjects and has grown steadily: from 129,274 exams in 2012 to 187,133 exams in 2019.[6] Therefore, leaving Spanish aside, we can focus on other foreign languages. Analyzing the data trend from 2012 to 2019 we can notice a constant increase in the number of exams taken.[7]

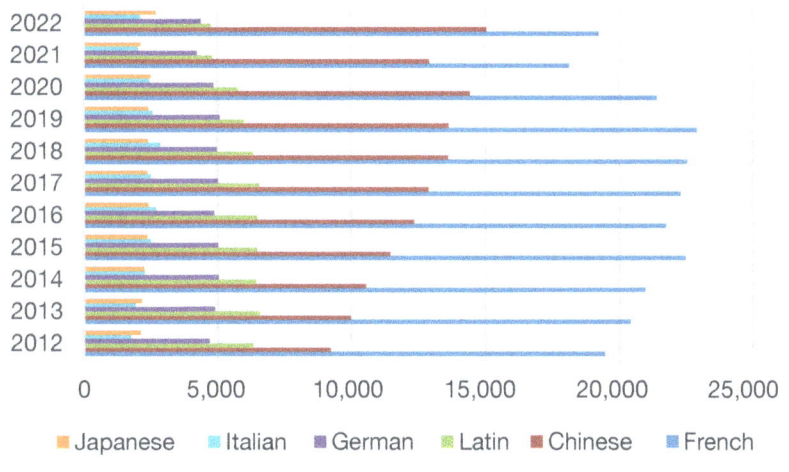

Chart 8: Foreign Language (except Spanish) AP exams. Period 2012-2022[8]

Chart 8 shows clearly that the other Foreign Languages can be divided in two groups. The first comprises French, that in the period considered is always around 20,000 exams and Chinese. In the other there are German, Latin, Italian and Japanese, ranging from around 5,000 to around 2,000. In the period considered only Chinese had a constant and considerable increase. It had grown by an average of about 7 percent every year, from 2012 until 2018, while from 2018 to 2019 it only maintained its quota (13,833 in 2019). AP French (23,249) in 2019 maintained a constant trend, even if with some fluctuation. German (5.160 in 2019), Japanese (2.479 in 2019), and Italian (2.658 in 2019) remained more or less constant, but having rather small numbers; for these languages even a minimal change is significant.

AP ITALIAN LANGUAGE AND CULTURE EXAM VOLUMES

In the previous section, we presented data regarding AP exams of all subjects and then isolated data on foreign language exams. We considered a relatively short period, 2012-2022, but large enough to allow us some remarks. I have noticed that there has been a general steady increase in the number of exams taken; that there are few fluctuations, apart from rare cases; that most exams focus on relatively few subjects as about a quarter of the subjects cover two-thirds of the exams; and that these particularly popular subjects are almost all from the humanities area. But in most recent years there is a faster increase in STEM subjects. I then isolated foreign languages where we noticed that Spanish is a case unto itself, as the numbers are not comparable with other foreign languages, and that all other languages, apart from French, are among the subjects with the lowest number of exams. Let us now take a closer look at the figures for Italian, the subject on which this study focuses.

As we saw in the previous chapter, the AP Italian Language and Culture Program was first proposed in 2006. Despite a good start, the College Board decided to suspend it in the years 2010 and 2011 because it had not met its planned targets. It was then re-proposed in 2012 thanks to an intense promotion and advocacy campaign by the community of Americans of Italian descent supported by the Italian government and other sponsors. Since then, with an average of 2,400 exams, AP Program in Italian consistently ranks last among all subjects in terms of the number of exams taken. In addition, Italian accounts on average for about 5 percent of the Foreign Languages AP exams, excluding Spanish; 1.1 percent if Spanish is included.

In greater detail, from 2006 to 2022, the figures for AP Italian Languages and Culture exam are the following:

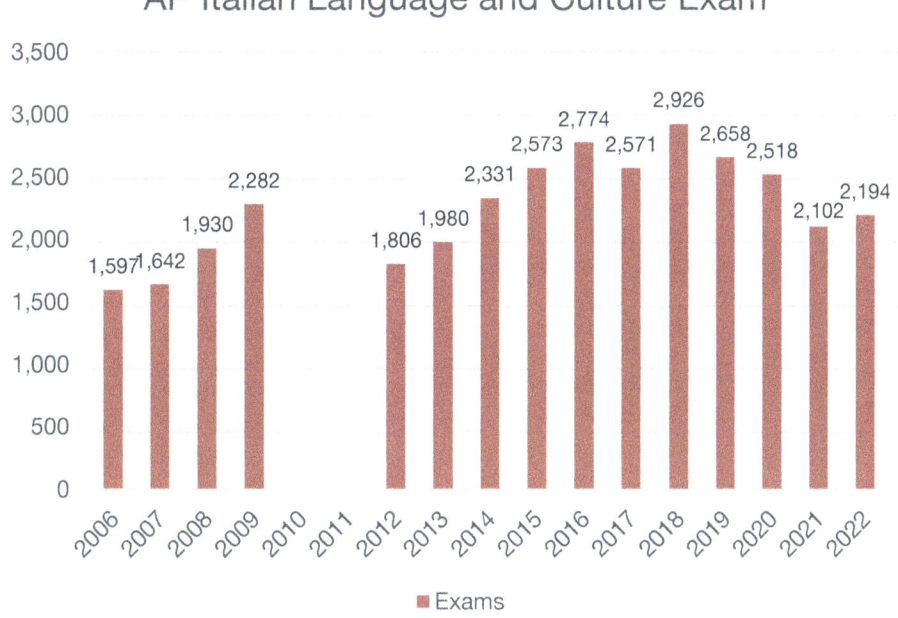

Chart 9: Number of students taking the AP Exam from 2006 to 2022

Even if the existence of the AP Italian Language and Culture exam is relatively short, resulting in insufficient information for a reliable trend analysis, some reflections can be drawn. From 2006 to 2022, the AP Italian Language and Culture Program increased from 1,597 a 2,194 exams: a 37 percent increase in 15 trials. It is noteworthy that the two-year interruption due to Covid 19 (2020–2021) was very traumatic for AP Italian. In fact, from 2006 to 2009 the AP Italian had an average growth of 13 percent. After the interruption, it was possible to bridge the gap and return to the 2009 figures only in 2014. From 2012 on, the numbers have grown at 6 percent on average, with a peak of 18 percent between 2013 and 2014. From 2016 on there is a swinging trend: a 7 percent drop between 2016 and 2017, a strong increase of 14 percent in 2018, which represents so far, the highest number achieved with 2,926 exams, followed by a 31 percent drop between 2018 and 2021 and an increase of 9 percent from 2021 and 2022.[9]

Students can take the exam at the school that offers it, even if it is not the school they regularly attend. Chart 10 shows the progress of schools offering AP Italian exam during the period 2006-2022:

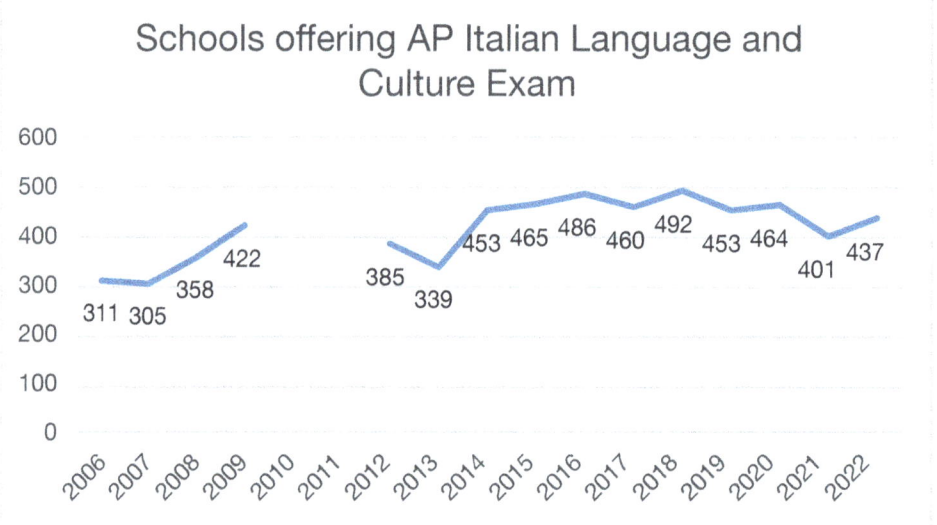

Chart 10: Schools offering AP exam 2006-2022.

"This represents the number of schools offering AP Exams to one or more students. Beginning in 2015, the number of schools include those that did not order or administer AP exams but had students who took the test at other schools. These schools were not included in prior years' counts" (College Board, collegeboard.org). The analysis of the chart must be divided into two parts, before and after 2015. In fact, as the College Board explains, if before 2015 only the schools that offered the exam were counted, after 2015 the number indicated includes the schools that "had students test at other schools."

As with the students, most schools are in the United States. For example, in 2019, thirty-three schools (or students coming from them) were in more than ten countries, from China to Dubai, South Africa, and Italy.

The data from the schools match those from students. There is still growth, but smaller: if the AP exam has recorded a constant increase of 6 percent from 2012 to 2019, schools (or students coming from different schools) show a growth by 3.2 percent. As for students, from 2019 to 2021, there was a decrease; and a small increase as well from 2021 to 2022.

THE AP PROGRAM DURING 2020 AND 2021

The pandemic had painful effects and consequences on everyone's life. It also disrupted the world of education, as everyone involved in it — from teachers to students to families — knows. The AP exam has certainly not been left out of this upheaval. The years 2020 and 2021, albeit in different ways, clearly attest to this.

If data analyzed in the previous paragraph show that there was a constant growth in general numbers, and in almost all subjects from 1956 on, in 2020 and 2021 the tendency is the opposite, and the reason is with no doubt linked to the pandemic.

The AP exam is administered in a controlled situation, with very strict protocols in order to ensure accuracy in results. The types of examination tests vary from subject to subject. Many involve answering multiple-choice questions; others also involve a practice test.

The foreign language exam consists of various tests, oral and written, aimed at assessing proficiency in foreign language and culture according to the guidelines set forth in the Course and Exam Description prepared by the College Board's team of experts.

As everyone certainly remembers, the 2019-2020 school year started regularly, but then from March 2020, due to the COVID-19 pandemic, class sessions were all moved online. Given the very serious health situation, the College Board decided that AP exam sessions, which are normally held in spring and summer in person, should also be held online. The College Board thus distributed an app that students had to download to their cell phones. They were thus able to take the exam from home.

All exam questions were reformulated and constructed so that they could be taken online. For foreign languages, the first part of the exam, the multiple-choice questions, had been suppressed. The exam consisted of two spoken tasks delivered on the smartphone app: a conversation task and a cultural comparison task. In the first task, students were to respond by following the instructions and recorded prompts, while in the second task, they were to listen to the instructions, prepare for four minutes, and record their presentation.[10]

The College Board made a truly remarkable effort to ensure that all students could take the exam despite the pandemic. It even provided make-up exams and worked hard to ensure that colleges would equally recognize the credits awarded for AP exams. But the administration of the AP exam still entailed a whole series of challenges, both organizational and technological, and there was no shortage of controversy. For example, precisely because of the online mode, the exam was held at the same time all over the world. As a result, some students had to take the test late at night. Several questions were also raised regarding the guarantee of fairness. Apart from the time difference, students could not all be under the same conditions. Some reported difficulties in accessing the Internet, while others reported not having a confidential enough place in which to take the exam. In the press, several articles reported class action suits by students who claimed that they had various technological problems which compromised their examination and security in the handling of personal data. Other complaints also accused the College Board of violating the Americans with Disabilities Act (Strauss 2020, Jaschik 2020, Snouwaert 2020).

In May 2021, the College Board changed the administration of the exam once more. First, some deadlines had been extended; for some subjects it was possible to take it online digitally, but with a computer and no longer through an app, at school or at home. For music and foreign languages, however, there was a return to the traditional mode of paper and pencil, apart from Chinese and Japanese, which were already offered in the online version.

Such a situation strongly influenced the numbers of students and exams taken in 2020 and 2021. Table 3 shows general data regarding students and exams in the last three years.[11]

Years	Students	Exams
2018-19	2,825,710	5,098,815
2019-20	2,642,630	4,751,957
2020-21	2,548,228	4,578,302

Table 3: Number of students and exams in years 2018-19 to 2020-21

From 2019 to 2021 the number of students taking an AP exam falls by more than 10 percent, and the total number of exams taken falls by more than 11 percent. It is the first time in almost seventy years. Concerning the specific subjects, Table 4 shows the trend for all 38 subjects in years 2019-2021

VARIATION OF SUBJECTS IN 2019, 2020, 2021						
	2019	Variat. 19-20	2020	Variat. 20-21	2021	Variat. 19-21
SPANISH LITERATURE & CULTURE	29,345	-18	24,137	-10	21,796	-28
ART & DESIGN: 3-D	6,040	-13	5,281	-13	4,573	-26
ITALIAN LANGUAGE & CULTURE	2,658	-5	2,518	-17	2,102	-22
FRENCH LANGUAGE & CULTURE	23,249	-7	21,701	-15	18,408	-22
PHYSICS 2	23,802	-8	21,835	-14	18,736	-22
SPANISH LANGUAGE & CULTURE	187,133	-10	168,998	-12	148,486	-22
PHYSICS C - E&M	25,342	-7	23,655	-13	20,471	-21
LATIN	6,083	-4	5,850	-16	4,889	-20
GOVT. & POL. - COMP.	23,522	-6	22,051	-13	19,292	-19
ART AND DESIGN: DRAWING	21,769	-6	20,486	-12	18,096	-18
EUROPEAN HISTORY	100,655	-6	94,312	-11	84,237	-17
CALCULUS AB	300,659	-11	266,430	-6	251,639	-17
ART HISTORY	24,476	-4	23,567	-12	20,633	-16
GERMAN LANGUAGE & CULTURE	5,160	-4	4,928	-12	4,315	-16
ENGLISH LITERATURE & COMP.	380,136	-12	333,980	-4	321,029	-16
STATISTICS	219,392	-14	187,741	-2	184,111	-16
PHYSICS 1	161,071	-7	149,488	-8	137,229	-15
CHEMISTRY	158,847	-8	145,540	-7	135,997	-15
PHYSICS C - MECH	57,131	-9	51,718	-6	48,803	-15
MACROECONOMICS	146,091	-16	122,639	1	124,436	-15
MUSIC THEORY	18,864	-12	16,550	-2	16,271	-14

MICROECONOMICS	91,551	-10	82,415	-3	80,199	-13
JAPANESE LANGUAGE & CULTURE	2,479	4	2,581	-15	2,204	-11
CALCULUS BC	139,195	-8	127,864	-3	124,599	-11
BIOLOGY	260,816	-10	233,444	-1	230,527	-11
ENGLISH LANGUAGE & COMP.	573,171	-7	535,478	-3	518,548	-10
GOVT. & POL. - U.S.	314,825	-7	293,196	-3	283,353	-10
U.S. HISTORY	496,573	-5	472,697	-4	454,204	-9
ART AND DESIGN: 2-D	37,749	-2	36,901	-6	34,509	-8
PSYCHOLOGY	311,215	-5	295,621	-2	288,511	-7
ENVIRONMENTAL SCIENCE	172,456	-6	162,469	-1	160,771	-7
HUMAN GEOGRAPHY	225,235	-3	218,333	-3	211,735	-6
CHINESE LANGUAGE & CULTURE	13,853	6	14,663	-11	13,122	-5
WORLD HISTORY	313,317	-3	302,942	0	302,232	-3
COMPUTER SCIENCE A	69,685	1	70,580	6	74,676	7
COMPUTER SCIENCE PRINCIPLES	96,105	21	116,751	0	116,466	21
SEMINAR	43,441	21	52,562	1	53,076	22
RESEARCH	15,724	28	20,055	20	24,021	48

Table 4. Trend for all 38 subjects. Years 2019 -2021

The Table reports that only four subjects — Research, Seminar, and Computer Sciences A and Principles — show positive trends in the years 2019-2021. Even though some subjects show an opposite shift in 2020 and 2021, the trend is clear: 34 subjects out of 38 go from -3 to -20 in 2021 with respect to 2019. The majority loss is at least 10 percent of the students, while subjects were subject to a decrease of 20 percent or more in two years.

If we focus our analysis on foreign-language shifts in 2020 and 2021, the negative trend is even more evident. In fact, all the languages lost more than 10 percent in two years, from -11 percent of Japanese to -22 percent of French, Italian, and Spanish Language and Culture, while Spanish Literature and Culture lost 28 percent in the same period. Chinese and Japanese undergo a different swing. In fact, in 2020 both show a rise of respectively +6 and +4 with respect to 2019; but in 2021, Chinese scored -11 percent and Japanese -15 percent with respect to the year before.

Thus, there is no doubt that the difference between 2020 and 2021 is most likely due to various factors, all linked to the pandemic, that affected both the exam itself and the attendance of classes during the two different school years, 2019-2020 and 2020-2021.

In summary, from 1956 to 2019 AP exams and students always showed a positive trend, in general, but also for every specific subject, even with some fluctuations. In the last two years 2020 and 2021 the numbers are negative. At first glance, it seems that the humanities have lost the most. A more careful analysis shows that the loss is distributed over all fields, from the humanities to the sciences, with no strong differences, except for foreign languages which have all lost substantially, with 5 AP Foreign Languages exam (6 if we consider Spanish Literature), among the ten subjects that lost more.

We should ask if the 2020 and 2021 situation due to the pandemic has left any traces afterwards as well. Right now, we only have the 2022 figures, and most likely it is too little to tell whether the trend has changed and whether it will last.

Let's look at the next table that focuses on foreign languages.

SUBJECT	2019	% Ch.	2020	% Ch.	2021	% Ch.	2022
CHINESE	13,853	6%	14,663	-11%	13,122	16%	15,277
FRENCH	23,249	-7%	21,701	-15%	18,408	6%	19,554
GERMAN	5,160	-4%	4,928	-12%	4,315	3%	4,450
ITALIAN	**2,658**	**-5%**	**2,518**	**-17%**	**2,102**	**4%**	**2,194**
JAPANESE	2,479	4%	2,581	-15%	2,204	25%	2,765
LATIN	6,083	-4%	5,850	-16%	4,889	-1%	4,832
SPANISH LAN.	187,133	-10%	168,998	-12%	148,486	5%	155,931
SPANISH LIT.	29,345	-18%	24,137	-10%	21,796	6%	23,009

Table 5 Difference in exams taken for AP Foreign Languages Exam, 2019-2022

As Table 5 shows, the data vary greatly from language to language. Chinese and Japanese have fully recovered their losses from 2020-2021, surpassing their 2019 numbers. The others, however, still have lower numbers than in 2019. In 2022, French is at -16 percent compared to 2019; Spanish is at -17 percent; German is at -13 percent; Latin continues to lose compared to 2021 and 2020 and is at -21 percent compared to 2019. Italian was among the languages, along with Spanish and French, to have lost the most in the pandemic years. In 2022, it recovered 4 percent compared to 2021, but is still at -18 percent compared to 2019.

The situation of AP Italian seems a bit worse than the other foreign languages. In fact, the negative trend already started in 2019 (-9 percent), after the peak of 2018. From 2018 to 2021 Italian lost 31 percent of exams taken, and even if in 2022 it has gained 4 percent, the performance in the period is the worst performance of all the foreign languages, apart from Latin. Actually, from 2020 to 2021, the performance of AP Italian is the worst of all the 38 subjects: -17 percent.

The figure of schools where AP Italian Language and Culture courses are offered during 2020 2021 reflects only in part the trend in the number of exams, as we see in Table 6:

	2019	%	2020	%	2021	%	2022
Italian Language	453	2%	464	-14%	401	9%	437

Table 6: Number of Schools offering AP Italian. 2019 -2020.

In 2019, the number of schools offering the exam had decreased by 8 percent compared to 2018, when the number of schools peaked at 492. But in 2019-2020 there is a small increase of 2 percent. The figure is not affected by the pandemic, as the school year began in fall 2019. But the pandemic certainly affected the number of schools offering the course in the 2020-2021 school year. In fact, there is a -14 percent, resembling the reduction in the number of exams. In the 2021-2022 academic year, the number of schools begins to rise again, with a significant increase of 9 percent from the previous year. This can be seen as a sign of strong vitality and commitment from both teachers and educational institutions, which, although not matched by the number of students, is promising for the future.

As we said earlier, the period analyzed does not allow us to tell whether this is a tendency over longer periods of time. Certainly, the pandemic was, we hope, an exceptional event. There remains the concern for Italian having a less strong recovery than other languages. Concern reinforced by the acknowledgement that it is a language already fragile in numbers. Perhaps its image as a language of culture rather than a "useful" language, an image that if it can be a strength, in times of crisis can become a point of weakness as even the trend of Latin seems to confirm.

I can add, however, that foreign languages have often been the disciplines that have suffered the most in times of economic or social crisis. When a feeling of closure to the outside world was widespread.

Toward a Profile for the AP Italian Language and Culture Student

In the previous paragraphs I presented the numbers of AP Italian Language Learning and Culture, concerning students, exams, and schools I analyzed the trend both since 2006, the year of the first AP exam, and since 2012, when AP Italian restarted after a two-year hiatus. It was clear that the AP Italian suffered a great deal from this interruption, but that from 2012 until 2018 the recovery was strong and steady, while from 2019 there was a reversal, which was exacerbated by the pandemic. The 2022 figure seems to manifest a small recovery, but we are still far from the 2018 numbers. I also mentioned that the reasons for this trend, apart from the pandemic period, are arguably multifaceted. For example, that foreign languages are the first to suffer from periods of crisis, whether economic, social, or, as in the case of the pandemic, of health. The fact that Italian is particularly perceived as a language of culture and therefore chosen for personal rather than professional reasons (Giovanardi and Trifone 2010; Dolci 2017; MAECI 2016, 2017, 2019), may have exacerbated this trend. However, it is certainly a sign of an underlying fragility, since the numbers of Italian are in general always quite small, since the peak in 2018 of not reaching three thousand, every small variation takes on an important implication for the survival of Italian.

In the following paragraphs we will analyze the data from a more qualitative point of view, trying to understand who the student is taking the AP Italian Language and Culture exam. The goal is always to have even more data to understand what strategy to set to promote it more and more effectively. As a methodology option, I decided to analyze and compare data over the period 2012-2019. I also decided not to compute in our analysis the AP Italian Language and Culture exam data for the period 2006-2009, since that experience was isolated due to the two-year interruption in 2010-2011.

I also decided to analyze partially data from 2020-2022 for the reasons expressed in the previous paragraph: that the pandemic represents an exceptional and hopefully unique event. Inclusion of data for those years would not allow for an analysis on the examinations for all allowed variables, which is what we are particularly interested in in this study.

Even though it is impossible to foresee the future trend of the Italian AP exam in the short term, we can attempt to understand if there is still room for growth or whether the program has reached its peak or whether the trend is downward instead.[12]

An important question is, for example, whether it is possible to increase the percentage of students that take the AP Italian Language and Culture exam with regard to the total number of U.S. high school students of Italian. Unfortunately, we have no recent data on the numbers of Italian students in the U.S. I could not find statistics on the number of Italian students in high schools after 2000,[13] while, at the K-12 level, the last survey available is dated 2008,[14] and it establishes the number of Italian language students in eighteen states at 78,273. The most recent statistics provided by the Italian Ministry for Foreign Affairs (MAECI) are not easily comparable, as they are not broken down by grade.[15] Moreover, the most recent and perhaps most accurate analysis of foreign languages in K-12, dated 2017, inexplicably does not include Italian (National K-12 FL Report, 2017).

Therefore, it is necessary, indeed urgent, that the stakeholders, institutions, associations, and the larger community that promote Italian in the U.S. unite in order to prepare an accurate and reliable survey able to provide consistent data on the number of students who take Italian at the different grades. Such data are essential for any kind of research and strategy on Italian Language in the USA.[16]

I will first analyze the distribution of the number of AP exams and courses within the U.S. territory. Again, we will rely on data provided by the College Board itself in its public reports. We will see that the distribution of exams and courses is clearly parallel and uneven, focusing on a few states. We will then try to find a rational for this distribution, which clearly seems to depend on the profile of the AP student. By cross-referencing the data offered by the College Board with those of other analyses, it becomes clear that for the most part the group of AP students is composed of students of more or less recent Italian origin and students of

Latinx ethnicity. I will then try to ask whether this result represents a strength or a weakness and what strategies can be developed to better promote the teaching of Italian language and culture in the US.

DISTRIBUTION OF AP ITALIAN LANGUAGE AND CULTURE EXAM IN THE USA

The first step of my analysis is to understand what the distribution of AP exams and courses is within states.

The College Board does not provide a detailed analysis for the international context, but only for the U.S. and Canada. But since the AP Italian Language and Culture exam is practically non-existent in Canada,[17] the analysis will solely focus on data concerning students and schools in the U.S., where the AP Program forms an integral part of the strategy concerning the promotion of the Italian language. Moreover, even at the general level, almost all AP Italian Language and Culture exams are held within the U.S., as the following table shows.

Exams USA	1,664	1,852	2,203	2,428	2,619	2,430	2,778	2,554	2,399
Exams Gen,	1,806	1,980	2,331	2,573	2,774	2,571	2,926	2,658	2,518
	2012	2013	2014	2015	2016	2017	2018	2019	2020

Table 7: Number of AP Italian exams in the US and around the world.

But AP exams are not evenly concentrated in the U.S. As we have already mentioned, within the North American context, the data show that participation in the Italian AP exam is not uniformly distributed throughout the U.S. It is concentrated in only a few states. The following data illustrate the situation in the students' home states for the years 2017, 2018, 2019, and 2020.

State	2017	2018	2019	2020	Aver.	State	2017	2018	2019	2020	Aver.
NY	796	1006	858	810	868	IA	5	1	1	1	2
NJ	444	520	590	481	509	IN	3	4			2
FL	260	205	237	188	223	NH	2	2	1	1	2
CA	175	196	205	150	182	NV	2		3	1	2
IL	192	179	168	173	178	LA		2	1	1	1
MA	166	189	157	176	172	NE	1	1	1	1	1
RI	71	95	84	75	81	TN	2	1		1	1
CT	46	63	52	64	56	MO		2	1		1
PA	41	41	56	48	47	HI		2		1	1
TX	51	48	36	47	46	OR		2		1	1
MD	41	42	51	39	43	VT		1		2	1
OH	33	48	12	59	38	KS			2	1	1
VA	22	34	17	20	23	MT	3				1
MI	27	20	12	9	17	OK		1		1	1
DE	10	4	6	12	8	WV				2	1
DC	1	12	9	9	8	UT	1			1	1
CO	5	16	7	1	7	SC		1			
NM	8	11	2		5	AK		1			
GA	4	5	5	4	5	ID		1			
WA		9	1	4	4	AR				1	
ME	5	2	3	4	4	KY				1	
WI	4	4	2	2	3	ND	1				
NC	2	1	4	5	3	SD					
AZ	3	3	2	2	3	WY					
MN	2	3	4		2	AL					
						MS					

Table 8: AP exam Students' home states in 2017, 2018, 2019, and 2020

The table clearly shows that only fourteen states had an average of ten exams per year in the 2017-2020 period. Another five states averaged between ten and five exams per year. About half of the states had two to zero students in the period under consideration.

If we consider a longer period, from 2012 to 2020, the figure does not change. The states with a significant presence of students taking the AP Italian exam are a strong minority.

States	2012	2013	2014	2015	2016	2017	2018	2019	2020
% of total exams	95%	96%	94%	95%	96%	95%	95%	95%	96%
NY	35,10	38,01	33,45	31,51	31,46	32,76	36,21	33,59	33,76
NJ	17,01	17,55	19,29	17,71	17,22	18,27	18,72	20,32	20,05
CA	9,74	7,56	7,35	8,11	8,86	7,20	7,06	8,03	6,25
FL	6,25	7,56	8,58	10,26	9,77	10,70	7,38	9,28	7,84
IL	8,35	7,51	6,22	8,20	8,63	7,90	6,44	6,58	7,21
MD	2,76	1,51	1,68	1,98	1,57	1,69	1,51	2,00	1,63
MA	6,19	6,91	6,58	6,26	7,29	6,83	6,80	6,15	7,34
OH	1,38	1,30	1,04	1,32	1,76	1,36	1,73	0,47	2,46
PA	1,44	2,43	1,86	2,55	2,02	1,69	1,48	2,19	2,00
RI	2,46	2,70	3,31	3,62	2,29	2,92	3,42	3,29	3,13

Table 9: Percentage of exams in most significant states

Table 9 shows that 95 percent of the exams are taken in 10 states and the percentage does not change over the 2012-2020 period. Only two states, NY and NJ, have over 50 percent of all exams.

This concentration may pose a problem. But before commenting on that situation, let us look at the data regarding the number of courses activated in the United States, another important figure for understanding the vitality of the AP Italian Language and culture exam.

THE AP ITALIAN COURSES VOLUMES

The AP exam is part of the AP Program, which consists of offering a course at the end of which the students can take the AP exam. We have previously analyzed the number of schools offering the opportunity to take the AP Italian Language and Culture exam. However, this number is relatively significant regarding the AP Italian Language and Culture Program's vitality. Much more significant in this regard is to analyze the number of courses (and most likely schools) that also offer an AP Italian Language and Culture course. In fact, the ratio of schools offering the student the opportunity to take the exam compared to those offering a course is about one to two.

For an AP course to be approved, a teacher (and a school) must submit a request to the College Board. The College Board writes:

> Any course that a school labels "AP" must receive authorization through a process called the AP Course Audit, which confirms the teacher awareness of the scope of the course and the occasional exam changes, and ensures that confidential practice exams and other resources are only accessible to real AP teachers verified by a school administrator. The course will be included in the AP Course Ledger — the official list of all AP courses — so colleges and universities can verify the student's transcript content.[18]

As is the case, a school that has received approval to activate a course may decide, for a variety of reasons, not to activate it. Therefore, the number of approved courses may differ from the number of AP courses offered.[19]

Again, the College provides, through its website, a ledger that represents the official list of the authorized AP courses for each year (AP Course Ledger).[20] The site can also display data on AP courses divided by Country and State.

Analysis of the AP Course Ledger offered by the College Board offers some interesting data. For example, from the 2011/2012 school year to the 2022/2023 school year as many as 479 different schools had at least one AP Italian Language and Culture course approved, while in the United States alone, the schools that had a course approved in 2011/2012 were 464. Table 10 shows the number of AP Italian Language and Culture Courses approved from 2011 to 2022 by the College Board.

	2011/2012	2012/2013	2013/2014	2014/2015	2015/2016	2016/2017	2017/2018	2018/2019	2019/2020	2020/2021	2021/2022
Total Courses	204	219	242	256	268	270	301	296	230	297	298
Total Students	1,806	1,980	2,331	2,573	2,774	2,571	2,926	2,658	2,518	2,102	2,194

Table 10: Number of AP Italian Courses authorized by the College Board Audit

According to Table 10, the schools that have been granted an approved AP Italian Language and Culture course show a steady and gradual increase from the 2011-2012 school year to 2020-2021. Over the said period, the average increase has been approximately 5 percent, with an oscillation between a significant peak of 11 percent between 2016-2017 and 2017-2018 and a minor decrease in 2018/19 with respect to the previous year. [21] In the same period, the number of students taking the AP Italian Language and Culture in the USA has increased by 3 percent on average. But if we narrow the analysis to the last 5 years, a worrying figure emerges. From 2017-2018 — year when the peak in the number of exams (2,926) and activated courses (301) — to 2021-2022, the number of activated courses has remained virtually unchanged. This is certainly a sign of vitality on the part of faculty and institutions. Nonetheless, there is a decrease of 7 percent.[22]

The data analyzed concerns the total number of AP Italian approved courses. If we focus on the US, the figure changes little. In fact, more than 95 percent of the courses and exams take place in the US territory. See the following table:

	2011/2012	2012/2013	2013/2014	2014/2015	2015/2016	2016/2017	2017/2018	2018/2019	2019/2020	2020/2021	2021/2022
Courses USA	204	219	242	256	268	270	301	296	223	292	291
Exams USA	1,664	1,852	2,203	2,428	2,619	2,430	2,778	2,554	2,399		

Table 11: Number of AP Italian Courses in the United States, 2011-2012 to 2021-2022

The table presents the number of AP Italian Language and Culture courses activated during 2011-2012 to 2021-2022 in the USA.[23]

The performance of courses approved, and exams taken in the U.S. is, clearly, the same as the general trend, but in the U.S. the numbers vary greatly from state to state and are concentrated in relatively few states, just as with the number of exams that was analyzed above, as we see in Table 12:

	2011/2012	2012/2013	2013/2014	2014/2015	2015/2016	2016/2017	2017/2018	2018/2019	2019/2020	2020/2021	2021/2022	2022/2023
AL	0		0	0	0	0	0	0	0	0	0	0
AK	0	0	0	0	0	0	0	0	0	0	0	0
AZ	0	0	0	0	0	0	0	0	0	0	0	0
AR	0	0	0	0	0	0	0	0	0	0	0	0
CA	12	13	15	15	15	16	17	18	18	17	15	16
CO	1	0	1	0	0	0	1	1	0	0	1	1
CT	7	9	11	11	9	9	10	8	9	10	11	11
DE	0	0	2	2	0	2	1	1	3	1	1	2
DC	1	1	0	0	0	0	0	0	0	1	0	0
FL	12	16	20	24	23	25	22	28	21	23	27	24
GA	0	0	0	0	0	1	1	1	1	1	1	1
HI	0	0	0	0	0	0	0	0	0	0	0	0
ID	0	0	0	0	0	0	0	0	0	0	0	0
IL	11	14	13	13	16	15	16	17	12	16	16	14
IN	0	0	0	0	0	0	0	0	0	0	0	0
IA	0	0	0	0	0	0	0	0	0	0	0	0
KS	0	0	0	0	0	0	0	0	0	0	0	0
KY	0	0	0	0	0	0	0	0	0	0	0	0
LA	1	1	1	1	1	1	1	1	1	1	1	0
ME	0	0	0	0	0	0	0	0	0	0	1	0
MD	6	5	5	6	6	6	8	7	4	9	7	5

MA	11	12	11	14	12	15	19	19	15	18	19	15
MI	1	3	3	3	3	3	3	2	0	1	1	1
MN	1	0	1	1	1	1	1	1	0	1	1	1
MS	0	0	0	0	0	0	0	0	0	0	0	0
MO	0	0	0	0	1	0	0	1	0	0	0	0
MT	0	0	0	0	0	0	0	0	0	0	0	0
NE	0	0	0	0	0	0	0	0	0	0	0	0
NV	0	0	0	0	0	0	0	0	0	1	1	0
NH	0	0	0	0	0	0	0	0	0	0	0	0
NJ	49	52	61	63	68	67	75	69	52	72	72	67
NM	2	3	2	3	1	2	2	1	0	1	1	1
NY	69	68	68	71	83	75	85	84	55	81	81	76
NC	1	1	1	1	0	0	1	0	1	2	2	1
ND	0	0	0	0	0	0	0	0	0	0	0	0
OH	3	3	3	3	3	4	4	4	4	4	4	3
OK	0	0	0	0	0	0	0	0	0	0	0	0
OR	0	0	0	0	0	0	0	0	0	0	0	0
PA	7	6	8	8	8	9	10	10	7	10	9	9
PR	0	1	1	1	2	2	4	5	3	5	5	5
RI	4	5	8	6	8	9	10	10	11	11	9	10
SC	0	0	0	0	0	0	0	0	0	0	0	0
SD	0	0	0	0	0	0	0	0	0	0	0	0
TN	0	0	0	0	0	0	0	0	0	0	0	0
TX	1	1	2	2	2	2	2	3	4	3	3	2
UT	0	0	0	0	0	0	0	0	0	0	0	0
VT	0	0	0	0	0	0	0	0	0	0	0	0
VA	0	0	0	1	1	1	1	1	1	1	1	1
WA	1	1	1	1	1	1	1	1	1	1	0	
WV	0	0	0	0	0	0	0	0	1	1	1	1
WI	0	0	0	0	0	0	0	0	0	0	0	1
WY	0	0	0	0	0	0	0	0	0	0	0	0

Table 12: Number of courses for U.S. states during 2012-2022

Table 12 shows that during the period 2011-2012 to 2021-22, twenty-five states have never activated a single course. In fact, about 95 percent of approved courses take place in only 12 states. Even more than 50 percent of the courses are concentrated in only two states: New York and New Jersey. The offering of AP Italian Language and Culture courses follows the same trend as the presence of AP students who have taken the exam: in fact, the states with no less than five AP Italian Language and Culture courses are only nine, as we have seen above. In any case, the trend over the 2011-2012 to 2022-2023 period shows a limited but constant growth, even with some variations.

Another significant figure that provides insight into the AP program's vitality is the ratio of the number of courses approved to exams taken, as shown in Table 13.

	2012	2013	2014	2015	2016	2017	2018	2019	2020	AV.
CA	14	11	11	13	15	11	12	11	8	12
CT	5	4	5	5	7	5	6	7	7	6
FL	9	9	9	10	11	10	9	8	9	10
IL	13	10	11	15	14	13	11	10	14	12
MD	8	6	7	8	7	7	5	7	10	7
MA	9	11	13	11	16	11	10	8	12	11
NJ	6	6	7	7	7	7	7	8	9	7
NY	8	10	11	11	10	11	12	10	15	11
OH	8	8	8	11	15	8	12	3	15	10
PA	3	8	5	8	7	5	4	6	7	6
RI	10	10	9	15	8	8	10	8	7	9
TX	34	27	20	20	34	26	24	12	12	23

Table 13: Ratio of number of students to number of courses in the most significant states

The ratio is always constant and settles around ten exams per activated course, with some special cases such as Texas, where in some years the ratio seems significantly higher than average. If we assume that the number of exams also corresponds to the number of students per class, we can say that ten students per class is a fairly good number. Both to ensure effective teaching, as necessary for a challenging course like AP, and to ensure the survival of the course itself. Interestingly, in the 2012-2020 period, the ratio does not change significantly. This testifies to a certain stability in the demand for, and thus the offer of, the AP Italian Language and Culture Program.

We have seen how in the U.S. the presence of both students and activated courses is, as one would expect, related. Indeed, the numbers analyzed show a very strong concentration. Such concentration may represent an issue. Furthermore, in some states, the AP exam's presence depends on a single if not very few schools. In such contexts, the presence of the AP Program in Italian is linked to occasional and, at times, seemingly unrelated factors, such as the individual effort of a single teacher and/or of a school principal. Having reliable data regarding the number of students taking the AP exam can help forecast the future of Italian teaching in given contexts. Then, comparisons of enrollments with the schools and colleges that offer Italian should help us better understand if greater coordination between schools and colleges can favor the offering of Italian courses in K-12 schools. However, to date, there is no institution or research center that collects this type of data.[24]

THE AP ITALIAN LANGUAGE AND CULTURE PROGRAM
AND ITALIAN ANCESTRY

Having seen in the previous section that the number of examinations and the number of courses is concentrated in only a few states, we will now try to understand why this distribution occurs.[25] As is already apparent at first glance, the states with the highest number of exams are those in which the highest number of people reporting to be of Italian ancestry are also concentrated.

This section will attempt to answer what the exact relationship is between an Italian/American community and the number of AP exams and courses in Italian Language and Culture and how this affects it. As reported by statistics updated to 2021, in the United States, nearly 16 million people claim to be Italian Ancestry, but only about 500,000 people claim to speak Italian at home. See the Table 14 below:

Rank	States	Italian Ancestry 2017	AP 2017 Ranking
1	NY	2,384,306	1
2	PA	1,433,860	11
3	CA	1,406,170	5
4	NJ	1,379,887	2
5	FL	1,188,927	3
6	MA	820,425	6
7	IL	732,575	4
8	OH	710,767	12
9	CT	597,056	9
10	TX	507,920	8
11	MI	454,930	13
12	VA	328,249	14
13	MD	305,482	10
14	RI	181,261	7

Table 14: States with population of Italian origin and AP exam ranking in 2017

Table 14 lists those states with more that 100,000 people with Italian origin in 2017.[26] The states are listed by ranking from the highest number of people to the lowest. Column three shows their dominant position in the 2017 AP Italian Language and Culture exams taken. As we can see, there is a clear correspondence between the states with a high population of Italian origin and the number of AP Italian exams. All the states on top of the list of Italian ancestry are in the list of top-ranking AP exams. Also, there is a notable correspondence between the two lists. For example, New York ranks first in both lists, and the position of the other states is almost the same in the two lists, although with some perceptible difference. Thus, we see that Pennsylvania is second according to Italian ancestry but only in eleventh place for AP exams taken; Ohio, in turn, is eight in the list of Italian ancestry yet twelfth for AP Italian exams taken. On the contrary, Rhode Island performs much better in the AP Italian list with respect to the Italian ancestry list. We can then affirm that a greater presence of Americans of Italian descent in a community corresponds a higher number of AP exams, save some exceptions.

Based on the above, some states obviously appear to perform better than others. A comparison of the numerical ratio of the population of Italian ancestry living in different states, to the AP exam, as shown in Table 7, appears to support such a conclusion, as we see in Table 15:

RI	2,553	DE	8,067
NY	2,995	TX	9,959
NJ	3,108	CT	12,979
IL	3,815	VA	14,920
FL	4,573	MI	16,849
MA	4,942	OH	21,538
MD	7,451	PA	34,972
CA	8,035		

Table 15: Ratio of students of Italian origin to the AP exams (More significant states)

Table 15 shows two extremes: Rhode Island, where the ratio is one AP exam per 2,553 people of Italian origin, and Pennsylvania, where the ratio is one AP exam to 34,972 people. This datum is important to understand where and if there is still room for improvement. If, for example, we could raise Pennsylvania's and Ohio's ratio to the same level as Massachusetts, we would have approximately 300 more students.

What are the reasons for such different behavior? I do not have a definitive answer to give. Perhaps some communities seem to be more aware of the importance of the presence of the Italian language in their curricula and more effectively promote the AP Program. Perhaps the heritage relationship with Italy does not pass through the language and therefore the pride in declaring oneself of Italian ancestry is not matched by the motivation to learn the language.

This hypothesis seems to be confirmed by other research more generally concerned with the teaching of Italian in schools and colleges in the US. A survey conducted by the John D. Calandra Institute at CUNY (Dolci 2017) shows that about 60 percent of Italian language learners at the K-12 level claim to be of Italian descent and that they study Italian as a heritage language. Unfortunately, however, the approximately 16 million Americans who claim to be of Italian descent are only matched by about 80,000 K-12 students.[27] As we mentioned earlier, the heritage bond is not only through language, but more generally through a sense of cultural heritage. Perhaps, targeting this pride of cultural belonging and turning it into motivation for learning Italian could be an effective strategy for a greater promotion of studying Italian.

Thus, we can conclude that the AP Italian exam and, more in general, the offer of Italian, still depends on the ancestry factor. At the same time, the data show that the learning of Italian as a heritage language might have considerable margins for growth.

Unquestionably, a favorable terrain for the increase of AP students is the presence of schools offering Italian courses at the high school level and throughout the K-12 curriculum, along with a good number of colleges that grant AP Italian credit. All this, however, requires effective coordination between high schools and colleges. Yet, even in this respect, the objective data necessary to bring the process to fruition are either unavailable or, if so, not up to date.

THE AP ITALIAN LANGUAGE AND CULTURE EXAM AND ETHNICITY

In the previous section I tried to show that a large proportion of the students who take an AP course and consequently take an AP exam are of Italian descent. However, these data were derived indirectly by analyzing the distribution of the number of exams and comparing it with that of those states where there is a larger presence of Americans of Italian descent. For this study, it might be useful to know what the profile of the remaining students is.

In this regard, the College Board provides some very interesting data relating to the ethnicity of AP students. The tables provided by the College Board divide students into six ethnicities: American Indian/Alaska native, Asian, Black, Hispanic, Native Hawaiian/Other Pacific Islands, and White.[28]

This breakdown provides some intriguing data regarding AP foreign language exams. For example, more than 70 percent of students taking AP Chinese Language and Culture and about 50 percent of those taking the AP Japanese Language and Culture exam claim to be Asian.[29]

For AP Language and Culture and AP Literature and Culture, the percentage of those who declare themselves Hispanic also reaches about 70 percent. In certain states, such as Texas, Florida, and California, the percentage can be as high as 80 percent.

As for AP Italian, students taking the exam are concentrated for the vast majority among white and Hispanic. See Table 16.[30]

	2012	2013	2014	2015	2016	2017	2018	2019
American Indian/Alaska native	0.0	0.0	0.1	0.3	0.1	0.2	0.2	0.0
Asian	5.0	3.8	3.6	4.1	2.2	4.1	4.6	5.1
Black	1.4	1.9	2.0	2.1	0.8	1.7	1.8	2.1
Hispanic/Latinx	23	24.6	26.4	23.9	28.8	30	27.4	.26.4
Native Hawaiian/Other Pacific Islanders	0.0	0.0	0.0	0.3	0.0	0.0	0.0	0.0
White	65.6	66.1	65.1	66.0	82.3	61.9	61.6	61.7
Two or more races	0.0	0.0	0.0	0.0	3.0	2.5	3.0	2.9
Other	0.0	0.0	0.0	0.0	0.0	0.1	0.0	0.0
No response	0.0	0.0	1.0	0.0	0.6	1.0	2.3	2.5
National Total	1,664	1,852	2,203	2,428	1,951	2,430	2,778	2,554

Table 16: AP Italian Exam 2012-2018. Percentage of race/ethnicity.[31]

The table shows that white and Hispanic/Latinx students represent the clear majority of all those who take the AP Italian exam. On average, white students comprise 66.3 percent of the group, while Hispanic/Latinx students amount to 23.3 percent. The presence of other ethnic groups is not notable. Asian students show some relevance, up to approximately 5 percent of the total in 2019. However, from 2012 to 2019, the percentage of white students decreases: from 65.6 percent in 2012 to 61.7 percent in 2019, while the Hispanic/Latinox presence goes from 21.9 percent in 2012 to 26.2 percent in 2019: such an increase is undoubtedly positive and should be encouraged.

The data also show that Asian and African American students are under-represented in the Italian AP Language and Culture exam, which would suggest the need for an effective promotional campaign aimed specifically at these ethnic groups.

As we have seen, AP Italian is present in a few U.S. states, and in even fewer of them do students write the examination in large numbers. Hence, an analysis of each state's data is not particularly significant, even though specific trends seem to emerge in the states where the AP students are concentrated.[32]

In California, White and Hispanic/Latinx experience a fluctuating trend. In 2016 Hispanic/Latinx reached its highest point, with 52.2 percent, but lost almost 10 points from 2016 to 2019 (41.5 percent). White is at its lowest point in 2018, with 36.6 percent, but rises to 42.9 percent in 2019. Asian reaches 8.5 percent in 2014, declines down to 3.9 percent in 2016 and rises back to 8.3 percent in 2019.

In Florida, students are 95 percent Hispanic/Latinx or White. From 2016 to 2017, there was a significant increase in Hispanic/Latinx students (73.8 percent) and a corresponding decrease in white students (21.9 percent). The trend of both remained constant since then, with a slight increase regarding the white students.

In states such as Illinois, Massachusetts, New Jersey, and New York, the gap between the two ethnic groups has remained strong, with no significant differences during the period analyzed.

In 2013, in Illinois, the gap between White (54 percent) and Hispanic/Latinx (42.4 percent) was minor; then it continuously increased as of 2017. In 2019 white reached 71.4 percent, as opposed to the Hispanic/Latinx 25 percent.

In Massachusetts, White students are constantly over 65 percent (75.8 percent in 2019) while Hispanic/Latinx students never exceed 25 percent (13.4 percent in 2019). Asian students reached 9.4 percent in 2016, to then decrease to 4.5 percent in 2019.

In New Jersey and in New York, the difference between White and Hispanic/Latinx has always been wide over the years. Hispanic/Latinx students are always around 20 percent, as opposed to Asian students reaching 7 percent in New Jersey and about 5 percent in New York. In 2019, Black students only reached the 3 percent level in the state of New York.

We can conclude that the large presence of Hispanic/Latinx students in high school represents an area with considerable potential, given the proximity between the two languages. It would help evaluate how many Hispanic/Latinx students who speak Spanish at home take the AP exam in at least two Romance languages. Plurilingual education and more inclusive learning methods, such as intercomprehension, could undoubtedly bring significant benefits to promoting the teaching of the Italian language in schools and to the AP Program.[33]

Notes

[1] Until 2014 the College Board published yearly an AP Report to the Nation. The links to the College Board sites with the data are listed in the Bibliography.

[2] This underscores that the downturn in the 2020-2021 two-year period is most likely due to the COVID-19 pandemic and not a trend reversal due to any other internal or external factors.

[3] All the sources of data can be found in the College Board website. They are cited in the bibliography.

[4] Generally speaking, the different trends of AP exams reflect the popularity of the corresponding disciplines throughout the U.S. school system. While still the "humanities" have the highest numbers, in recent years, the greatest growth is in the STEM disciplines, corresponding with an increasing emphasis given by educational policy to these topics.

[5] Latin focuses on the in-depth study and translation of selections from Virgil's *Aeneid* and Caesar's *Gallic War*.

[6] The status of Spanish as a Heritage language is clearly demonstrated by the fact that the majority of students taking the AP Spanish Language and Culture exam in the U.S. are of Hispanic/Latinx origin, peaking at 69 percent in 2019. Also, in certain areas of the U.S., as is well known, the popularity of Spanish is such that the very term "Foreign Language" is called into question.

[7] Let us not forget member that the College Board also offers an exam in English Language and Composition and English Literature and Composition. As previously shown, in 2019 they represented respectively 11.2 percent and 7.5 percent of the total AP exams taken in all subjects. In fact, these are among the most requested ones. Even though for a certain number of students English might be a foreign language, in this research we do not consider it as such.

[8] Until 2009 the College Board offered an exam in French literature and another in Latin literature. Since 2013 the Latin-Virgil and Latin exams have been merged.

[9] The AP is an international exam and can therefore be taken not only by students of other nationalities, but also in other schools outside the United States. But the vast majority of students and schools are on US soil. In fact, during the period 2012-2019 the percentage of students taking the exam outside the USA ranged from 9 percent in 2012 to 4 percent in 2019, with an average of 6 percent.

[10] *College Board, 2020 AP Testing Guide*. Retrieved March 2021.

[11] Actually, the number of schools has a different trend. In fact, while in 2018-2019, 22,678 schools offered the AP exam, in 2019-2020, before the pandemic, there were 22,152 (-2 percent), while in 2020-2021, during the pandemic, the number reached its peak with 22,802 schools (+3 percent).

[12] We saw above that this is the opinion of the president of AATI who was AP exam Chief Reader from 2013 to 2016.

[13] ACTFL (American Council of Teachers of Foreign Language) (2002). *Foreign Language Enrollments in Public Secondary Schools*, Fall 2000. ACTFL.

[14] ACTFL (American Council of Teachers of Foreign Language). (2008). *Foreign Language Enrollments in K–12 Public Schools: Are Students Prepared for a Global Society?* Alexandria (VA): ACTFL.

[15] For example, the report by MAECI (2018) states that there are 221.741 students of Italian in the U.S. 46.475 are in "local schools" without any other specification.

[16] As is well known, the MLA provides this kind of data for college and university. Ironically, from 1922 to 1939 Mario Cosenza, president of ITA (Italian Teachers Association), was able to collect reliable data, even using the regular mail, the only "technology" at his disposal at that time.

[17] According to the College Board, in Canada three students took the AP exam in 2018, one in 2019, four in 2020. The reason for this trend, in a context historically rich of heritage speakers, would deserve a separate analysis.

[18] https://apcentral.collegeboard.org/courses/ap-course-audit/about.

[19] This actually happens in very few cases and only for a few school years. In fact, the number of courses approved is then the number of courses actually implemented.

[21] The data for the 2019/2020 school year appears to be inconsistent. In fact, data from the AP Course Ledger shows that in the 2019-2020 school year there was a sharp drop from 296 to 223 schools, a remarkable -22 percent from the previous year. The figure appears to be insubstantial for two reasons, the first because the number of exams, and thus most likely the number of students taking courses, only dropped by 5 percent. Moreover, in the following year, 2020-2021, the number of courses offered has recovered to the figures of 2018-2019.

[22] The figure is definitely affected by the effect of the pandemic. Therefore, one will have to wait another year or two to better understand what is happening. But the figure should function as a wake-up call, since the number of exams has been well below the 2,500 mark for two years now. Another worrying figure, if correct, is the number of courses approved in 2022-2023 according to the AP Course Ledger, which is 276. -7 percent from the previous year.

[23] Unfortunately, the data for US exams in the year 2021 and 2022 are not available on the College Board website. There also remains a significant problem of inconsistency for the AP course data for the 2019/2020 school year.

[24] Also, notice that at the college level Italian lost 30% of students from 2009 to 2016, as the MLA reports show (Goldberg, Looney and Lusin 2015; Looney, and. Lusin 2019).

[25] Data taken from http://data.census.gov retrieved September 2022.

[26] Ancestry data are taken from: https://www.census.gov Retrieved November 2019

[27] Unfortunately, the figure is from 2008 and there are no more recent data at this time. (ACTFL 2008).

[28] It is also possible to to declare oneself as "two or more races."

[29] So not necessarily Chinese or Japanese. Let us remember that the numbers of AP Chinese and AP Japanese are very different. AP Chinese is supported by about 10,000 students each year, while AP Japanese by about 2,000 students.

[30] The College Board cautions against comparing data before 2015 with the most recent data. In particular, those who from 2016 onwards are defined as *Hispanic/Latinx* students were divided into *Mexican/American, Other Hispanic*, and *Puerto Rican* until 2015. In order to compare the data from 2012 to 2018, we decided to merge these last three different categories into the Hispanic/Latinx voice. It should also be remembered that the numbers refer to exams taken in US schools, thus excluding international students.

[31] There is an error in 2016 data.

[32] Only states with an average of 5 percent of AP exams over the 2012-2019 period are analyzed. Only ethnic groups that have at least 1 percent on average over the 2012-2019 period are analyzed. Two or more races is not included.

[33] For a discussion on Plurilingualism and Intercomprehension as assets for teaching Italian in the USA, see Dolci and Tamburri (2015). See also Wright,. Boun, and Garcìa (2015).

CHAPTER 3
THE ANALYSIS OF THE AP ITALIAN COURSE AND EXAM

INTRODUCTION

In the first part of this chapter, we will quickly introduce the AP Program, its purpose and philosophy, that is, which educational principles it follows. We will then describe how it is structured, and how it is constantly monitored. We will then present in greater detail the AP Italian Language and Culture Program following the course and exam description that guides teachers and students in the implementation of the course and exam preparation, ensuring a shared standard that guarantees the quality of the educational intervention. We will then describe the AP Italian Language and Culture exam and its structure.

In the second part, we will instead analyze students' scores on the AP Italian Language and Culture exams. In particular, we will focus on the second part of the exam, which is called Free Response Questions. Once again relying on data provided by the College Board. Finally, I will analyze the Chief Reader Reports.

Every year the AP's Chief Reader writes a report on the exam where he/she examines the results of the Free Response Questions, but more importantly, he/she provides valuable guidance to teachers on how to intervene to improve student performance by making the best use of the instructional students provided by the College Board, first and foremost the course and exam description.

This study will analyze some the reports and try to answer to the question if and how they have been received by the teachers. They might give some hints about the relationship between the AP Course and the AP exam, and how to improve it. This involves all the stakeholders: teachers, administrators, students, families, and the community.

THE AP ITALIAN PROGRAM

As we know, the Advanced Placement Program allows thousands of students to earn college credits through taking a specific course while they are attending high school. For the course to be recognized and thus give credit, it must be structured like a college course, both in terms of content and the development of critical skills, analytical skills, and argumentation. All skills typical of a college level course. At the end of the course, all students take an exam, normally held in May, which certifies exactly the achievement of the skills developed in the course and thus allows them to prove that the course is equivalent to one offered at the college level.

To ensure the validity of the course and exam, the College Board creates a Developing Committee composed of AP teachers and college faculty who control all stages of the process: they approve the syllabi proposed by the AP teacher, prepare the exams, and correct them.

Close cooperation among these experts and continuous discussion with stakeholders (principals, teachers, families, civil society representatives, etc.) ensures the validity and reliability of the entire process.

Approval of the syllabus is the most important part of the process. As the College Board says, the content and goals of the syllabus were determined after an analysis of hundreds of Italian language syllabi offered at the college level: to ensure that the objectives of the AP syllabus match those of a syllabus in an Italian course offered in colleges or universities.

The AP Italian Language and Culture Course is essentially based on the development of communicative and cultural skills and their use in real-life situations, thus trying not to "overemphasize grammatical accuracy at the expense of communication." The College Board states that the AP Italian Language and Culture Course is "approximately equivalent to an upper-intermediate college or university course in Italian Language and Culture."[1]

The College Board, respecting school and teacher autonomy, ensures that each of them can design their own curriculum and syllabi. But to ensure maximum transparency and validity of the process, any school or teacher who wants to offer an AP course must follow pre-established procedures that are defined in the AP Course Audit.[2]

The AP Course Audit is used to ensure that the course proposed by the AP teacher ensures that the curricular objectives defined by the AP level are met, and therefore that the proposed content, activities, and materials are adequate to ensure that the student can take the final exam and achieve at least the minimum score to earn college level credits.

The main requirement is, therefore, to enable the student to develop the skills and achieve the objectives described in the Course Description for Italian:

- The teacher uses Italian almost exclusively in class and encourages students to do likewise.
- The course provides opportunities for students to engage in interdisciplinary course content and develop skills through the 6 required themes: Families and Communities, Personal and Public Identities, Beauty and Aesthetics, Science and Technology, Contemporary Life, and Global Challenges.
- The course provides opportunities for students to demonstrate an understanding of the products, practices, and perspectives of the target cultures.
- The course provides opportunities for students to make cultural comparisons.
- Instructional materials include a variety of authentic audio, visual, and audiovisual sources and authentic written texts.[3]

Furthermore, the teacher and the school must ensure that all students who will take the course have access to all materials used, both in the classroom and at home, and the necessary technology equipment to properly use all audio and video and digital materials.

The College Board does not give any specific guidance on which materials to choose or textbooks to adopt, leaving it up to the teacher to identify the most appropriate ones to meet the required curricular requirements.

But the College Board provides many aids to the teacher: sample syllabi, sample activities, expert advice, participation in a community of practice in which to exchange ideas and best practices, and even training courses.[4]

THE AP ITALIAN COURSE DESCRIPTION

From 2005 to date, the College Board has published three course descriptions of the AP Italian Language Course and exam. The three Course Descriptions all share the same approach and are based on the ACTFL *Standards for Foreign Language Learning in the 21st Century* which were originally published in 1996 and have gone through various revisions and updates up to the latest version in 2015 called *World Readiness Standards for Learning Languages*.

Throughout the years, the ACTFL Standards have become the most important tool on which foreign language curricula at the K-16 level in the U.S. are based. They have influenced the design of textbooks and foreign language proficiency certificates. Over the years they have aligned and compared with other education standards in the U.S., such as the Common Core Standards and 21st Century Skills.

The framework and approach of the ACTFL standards are still the same, as described by the statement of philosophy, originally drafted in 1996 and revived in 2015:

> Language and communication are at the heart of the human experience. The United States must educate students who are equipped linguistically and culturally to communicate successfully in a pluralistic American society and abroad. This imperative envisions a future in which ALL students will develop and maintain proficiency in English and at least one other language, modern or classical. Learners who come from non-English-speaking backgrounds should also have opportunities to develop further proficiencies in their first language. (2015, 7)

As is well known, the standards are organized around five areas, or goals, that constitute foreign language education, commonly now known as the five Cs: Communication, Cultures, Connections, Comparisons and Community.

The 2015 revision is not only the result of ever-increasing coordination with other educational standards. It is also the result of a long process of experimentation and discussion among all stakeholders since their first publication in 1996. The 2015 version places emphasis precisely on the importance of world languages knowledge as an essential part of each student's global competence. World language knowledge interconnects and integrates even better with the proficiency in other disciplines. All these skills together form the literacy necessary to be ready to cope with the challenges of the globalized world. To achieve this very goal, the *World Readiness Standards for Language Learning* emphasize more clearly than previous versions the need to develop critical thinking skills and creativity in learning a foreign language:

The Standards have explicitly added attention to the development of literacy and the 21st century skills of communication, collaboration, critical thinking, and creativity. (2015, 17)

The increasingly interconnected dimension among the five goal areas is also emphasized, as exemplified in the revised version of the 5Cs logo. In fact, whereas in the 1996 logo the five circles representing the five areas intersect, in the *World Readiness Standards for Language Learning* logo the circles do not close in on themselves, but rather connect to each other, thus emphasizing the idea of interconnectedness between the various areas. They also surround a stylized globe, emphasizing the need for a global approach. The very decision to change the original name from *Standards for Foreign Language Learning in the 21st Century* to *World-Readiness Standards for Learning Languages* represents this global and interconnected dimension and the need to be prepared for the challenges of the future where languages will no longer be "foreign" but will be part of each person's educational and professional background.

Communication is clearly at the heart of foreign language teaching and learning. The *Standards* identify three modes of oral and written communication: interpretive, interpersonal and presentational. Each mode involves a particular link between the language and the underlying culture that develops gradually over time. At the foundation of this framework lies the knowledge of the language system that underpins the entire framework: "The use of the grammatical, lexical, phonological, semantic, pragmatic, and discursive features necessary for participation in the three communicative modes" (2015, 33).

The AP Italian Language and Culture Course and Exam Description incorporates the vision of the *World Readiness Standards for Language Learning* when it points out in the introduction how:

In today's global community, competence in more than one language is an essential part of communication and cultural understanding. [...] Advanced language learning offers social, cultural, academic, and workplace benefits that will serve students throughout their lives. The proficiencies acquired through the study of languages and literatures endow language learners with cognitive, analytical, and communication skills that carry over into many other areas of their academic studies. (2020, 11)

The 2020 course description, just like the precedent ones, states that the AP Italian Language and Culture course takes a holistic approach to language proficiency. Integrating the linguistic features of the language with communication strategies and cultural awareness. The description reaffirms again that in the classroom the focus is on function and not on form "avoiding overemphasis on grammatical accuracy at the expense of communication." (2020, 11)

Although the basic principles are the same, there are significant differences between the 2011 Course Description and the 2019/2020 Course Description. The 2020 Course Description has a very structured framework that was also created with the intent of providing strong structure support to teachers by giving them the most appropriate tools to construct a syllabus that is aligned with course objectives and adequate to properly prepare students to take the final exam. The College Board's intent to support the AP teacher's work even better is demonstrated by the same number of pages in the Course Description, which increases from 70 in 2011 to 198 in 2020.

In fact, although the teacher is free to choose and set the syllabus, he or she deems most suitable, the entire framework is aimed at helping the teacher construct motivating lessons with a meaningful context and aimed at providing the student with the best opportunities to develop the skills needed to adequately tackle the exam. The thematic approach is exemplified in six thematic units that provide the teacher and student with all the stimuli needed to "investigate and express different views on real world issues, make connections to other disciplines and apply skills and perspectives across content areas" (2020, 15). An important part in each unit is devoted to task models that help the student become familiar with the exam.

The course framework consists of four different strands: the first is the Skills, "which identify what students should know and be able to do to be successful in the course." These skills are four for the interpretive mode: (1) Understanding the text; (2) Making cultural and interdisciplinary connections; (3) Interpreting the text, that is, interpreting the meaning of a text and its features; and (4) Making meaning, that is, determining the meaning of words and using them appropriately for a given context.

The Interpersonal mode is represented by two skills that interpret the student's ability to understand and apply appropriate communicative strategies and syntactic expressions in oral and written interaction with others.

The ability to plan, to use appropriate vocal, written, and visual strategies, along with appropriate linguistic expressions, are the skills to be developed in the Presentational mode.

The second component includes the course themes, that are the same as the precedent course descriptions: Families and Communities, Global Changes, Contemporary life, Beauty and aesthetics, Science and technology. This thematic approach provides context and content for students to develop their skills in the modes of communication, the foundation of the course, as underlined by the Course Description. The Course is organized into precisely these six thematic units that provide a context for authentic, engaging activities that are responsive to students' interests. The Course Description reiterates that the teacher can construct the thematic path as he or she pleases, but it assures the teacher that the proposed thematic path guarantees that all themes are adequately addressed, and all modes of communication are equally practiced. Ultimately, that the student can adequately prepare for the exam.

The most innovative part of the 2020 Course Description, compared to 2011, is the list of thematic units accompanied by the unit guide that accurately describes the steps, the essential questions, and the techniques for building the course skill to engage the student with written, print, visual, audio visual and audio texts. The Unit Guide also contains Stimuli/Task models structured like those that students will find on the exam, to provide them with practice in each unit to properly address the tasks that form the AP exam.

After the description of the thematic units, the Course Description describes the Achievement Level Descriptors (ALDs) that define how well students at each level perform. The ALDs are described in five levels, like those on the exam, and are useful for both teachers and students to understand the level achieved in the various skills and to plan how to get to the next level (2020, 115). The ALDs are calibrated following the *ACTFL Performance descriptors for language Learners*.

The Course Description then devotes a chapter to Instructional Approaches with advice to teachers on how to select and use the teaching materials, what are the most effective teaching strategies to use to effectively address the productive and receptive skills and those concepts that the students will find at the exam. Finally, the final chapter outlines in detail the exam and its parts, how student learning is assessed on the AP exam, and some example exam questions.

It is clear from this brief description how the Course Description provides a strong and reliable structure for the teacher to help him or her organize effective teaching. It also clearly emerges how the course and the exam are closely related and share the same principles and objectives. Therefore, it is important for the teacher, even in his freedom, to know it well and draw inspiration from it. We will see later that Chief Reader Reports often point out this need.

THE AP ITALIAN EXAM

The AP program requires that at the end of the AP course the student take an exam that verifies achievement of the objectives set out in the course. Passing this exam is a necessary condition for the student to have recognized college credits.

Just as with the course, close collaboration between schoolteachers and college faculty is therefore necessary for exam preparation. Collaboration is ensured by the composition of the AP Test Development Committee. The exam consists of two parts. The first is a series of closed-ended, multiple-choice questions and is automatically corrected. The second, on the other hand, consists of open-ended questions. This second part is corrected by a team of specialists, led by the Chief Reader, who ensure compliance and alignment with the decided standards.

As the College Board points out, AP Exams are not norm-referenced, i.e., they do not describe the student's performance in comparison to the performance of students in the norm group, but rather are Criterion reference, i.e., based on a predetermined reference standard. So, the individual student's grade isn't calculated according to the performance of their peers, as in norm reference tests, but rather on a predetermined standard, or criterion. That criterion is based, as the CB reports, on:

- The number of points successful college students earn when their professors administer AP Exam questions to them.

- The number of points researchers have found to be predictive that an AP student will succeed when placed into a subsequent, higher-level college course.
- Achievement-level descriptions formulated by college faculty who review each AP Exam question (2020, 2).

The scores of the two sessions are then carefully weighed and combined and then converted into a scale ranging from 1 to 5 according to the following classification:

5. Extremely well qualified
4. Well qualified
3. Qualified
2. Possibly qualified
1. No recommendation

Colleges and universities can decide for themselves what recognition to give to credit scores, but it is now widespread policy to award credit starting at level 3.[5]

THE STRUCTURE OF THE AP ITALIAN LANGUAGE AND CULTURE EXAM

The AP Italian Language and Culture exam is aimed at assessing to what level the student has developed the skills that are the goal of the course syllabus, for which there is a very strong relationship between the syllabus and the exam. In fact, for each Course Description in force since 2006 there corresponds a different exam structure and content, at least in part.

The first version of the AP Italian Language and Culture exam was offered from 2006 to 2009. When the AP Italian Program was offered again after being discontinued in 2010 and 2011, a new Course Description was adopted to which the exams from 2012 through 2019 were linked. From fall 2019, the third Course Description came into effect; but the 2020 exam, due to the pandemic, is was completely rewritten. So, the 2019 new Course Description was linked to the 2021 and 2022 exams.

While the three versions maintain a similar general structure of multiple-choice questions and open-ended responses, they differ on the weight to be given to each of the sections. In addition, although all course descriptions are based on the ACTFL Standards and the three Communication Modes — Interpretive, Interpersonal, Presentational — the competencies, skills, and objectives are somewhat different, and this is partly reflected in the exam. The duration of about three hours remains the same for all three versions of the exam.

In the 2006 and 2011 versions, the three modes of communication and culture were assessed separately from each other. For example, the structure of the 2006 exam included a test to assess listening and reading through 70 multiple-choice questions, whereas section II assesses Writing, and Speaking, with a variety of questions from paragraph completion to composition. Cultural knowledge was assessed through a composition in Italian on a cultural topic. There is still a strong accent on assessing grammar with specific tasks like paragraph completion in section II part A. Each section is given the same weight of 20 percent of the total.

Instead, the 2011 version represents a definite step forward by integrating the three communication modes even though they were still assessed separately. Specifically, grammar was evaluated into the task measuring the communication modes. Interpersonal writing mode was assessed trough the specific task of writing an e-mail. Culture, in turn, was not evaluated separately, but a cultural topic is a stimulus for speaking in the interpersonal mode. More specifically, the structure of 2011- 2019 exam, which is the main part of our analysis, consisted of:[6]

- 80-minute multiple-choice questions and 85-minute free-response section. Both accounted for half of the student's exam.
- Section I assessed Interpretive Communication mode by asking students to identify the main ideas, details, and purpose of a variety of audio and written texts. It consisted of 70 multiple-choice questions, almost evenly divided.
- Section II assessed interpersonal and presentational communication with four different tasks asking for free response questions.

The three modes of communication are assessed in more integrated forms in the structure of the 2019 AP Italian Language course and exam description. The course description states explicitly that the assessment phase also takes a holistic approach.

Confirming the close connection with the Course Description, the exam will assess the themes and skills developed in each of the six Units presented in the Course Description (2020, 163):

1. Families in Different Societies
2. The Influence of Language and Culture on Identity
3. Influences of Beauty and Art
4. How Science and Technology Affect Our Lives
5. Factors That Impact the Quality of Life
6. Environmental, Political, and Societal Challenges

This exam also consists of two sections. The first is divided into two parts. Part A has 30 questions and counts toward 23 percent of the total. Part B has 35 questions and counts 27 percent of the total. The second section (Section II) consists of four tasks. The two sections are weighted the same way: 50 percent of the total score.

"All eight AP Italian Language and Culture skill categories are assessed on every AP Exam in the multiple-choice and free-response sections" (2020 Course Description, 164). Specifically, the skills Comprehend Text, Make Connections, Interpret text, and Make Meanings are assessed in both the first and second sections. In the first section a literary text, an article, an interview, instructions, etc. represent different stimuli to which question sets are assigned. The second session integrates the assessing of these skills with those that belong to the creative and productive competence of language: Speak to Others, Write to Others, Present Orally, and Present in Writing. These skills are assessed through four different tasks: an e-mail reply, an argumentative essay, a conversation, and an oral presentation of a cultural topic. Each question assesses the student for a specific ability but also using a holistic scale that assesses her/his ability to maintain the exchange, provide the required information, communicate in a clear and understandable manner in the formal register, using appropriate and varied grammar, syntax, and sentence structure use of the appropriate linguistic features, etc....[7]

More specifically, the e-mail replay requires students to compose an e-mail reply in the formal register in response to an incoming e-mail in Italian, thus assessing the student's ability to provide the required information with details and elaboration. The argumentative essay task assesses student's ability to present and defend his/her position on a topic by writing an essay. The conversation task requires students to participate in a simulated discussion with a recorded interlocutor and specifically assesses speaking features, that is, the students' ability to use appropriate pronunciation, intonation, and pacing to enhance comprehension. Cultural Comparison requires students to distinguish an aspect of an Italian-speaking community with which they are familiar, to that in their own or another community. In performing this task students will demonstrate their ability to compare their own culture with the Italian one and their ability to understand it.

Each year, the College Board publishes statistical analyzes on the final scores achieved, and on the session II Free Response Questions in particular. In addition, the Chief Reader draws up a report on the exam and its results. Then he/she writes a series of recommendations and advice to the teachers based on the analysis. He/she also suggests in which aspects of the curriculum they should intervene in order to make their work even more effective.

The Analysis of the AP Italian Scores

As we have seen so far, the College Board pursues a policy of transparency about the AP exam both to the student and families as well as to the teacher. In this regard, it provides a great deal of information about both the course and the AP exam to make the student and families aware of what an AP course is and thus enable them to prepare as well as possible. At the same time, it provides support and assistance to teachers through the materials made available to them. The student can find on the AP Italian Language and Culture webpage a description of the course objectives ("Skills you'll learn"). These emphasize that he/she will learn to use language and learn about culture in order to communicate in real-world contexts and with authentic materials. The student learns that the course is intermediate level (typically third- or fourth-semester Italian), and that there are no prerequisites to enroll, although the course is normally offered in the fourth year of high school. The College Board states that for native speakers or heritage speakers, the course may be different. The page also describes the content of the six units into which the course is divided, and for each one it lists the language and cultural content and objectives, which are presented through the activities the student will practice.

On the exam page the student can find a detailed description of the different sections of the exam, with the types of texts used, the duration of each section, the number of questions, the value of each section for the final grade.[8]

The page for teachers is divided into various sections containing course and exam descriptions, teaching resources, sample syllabi to help prepare one for submission to the course audit, information on professional learning, etc. The page reserved for the exam, in turn, describes the contents, methods, and purposes of the various sections.[9]

With a very detailed description, special attention is given to the second part of the exam, The Free Response Section. See Table 17:

Exam Questions and Scoring Information

2022: Free-Response Questions

Questions	Scoring	Samples and Commentary	Audio Samples
Free-Response Questions	Scoring Guidelines	**Interpersonal Writing**	**Interpersonal Speaking Samples**
AP Italian Language 2022 Audio Scripts	Chief Reader Report	Email Reply	Student Sample 3A
	Scoring Statistics	**Presentational Writing**	Student Sample 3B
Speaking Audio Prompts	Score Distributions	Argumentative Essay	Student Sample 3C
		Interpersonal Speaking	**Presentational Speaking Samples**
		Conversation	
		Presentational Speaking	Student Sample 4A
		Cultural Presentation	Student Sample 4B
			Student Sample 4C

Table 17: The Exam and Scoring Information section for the 2022 Free Response Questions

This section is particularly useful for the teacher and presents an in-depth analysis of the section of the exam devoted to testing student's ability in Interpersonal and Presentational Speaking and Writing. The Questions column publishes the questions for the relevant year, the scripts and the speaking audio prompts. Such tools are certainly very useful for the teacher to practice with students on exam papers. The Samples and Commentary column presents examples of student productions with the grade achieved and the examiners' comments. This part is important because the examiners' comments provide insight into how the evaluative criteria for the exam are applied. Such criteria can be adopted by teachers themselves when they have students practice exam preparation. Audio samples — original student productions during the exam — can also be particularly useful. Each of these examples is accompanied by the score it received on the assessment. The example can then be used by the teacher as a comparative model for student productions, and it can also be used, for the same purpose, by the students themselves. The Scoring column shows the Guidelines, which describe the guidelines for each of the scores, from 1 to 5 that can be assigned to the student's response for individual questions. For example, the e-mail reply is given a score of 1 if it is "Barely understandable, with frequent or significant errors that impede comprehensibility." While a score of 5 is awarded if it is "Fully understandable, with ease and clarity of expression; occasional errors do not impede comprehensibility." This example is just one of the criteria used to score the various tests. The guidelines also include other criteria, such as richness of vocabulary, organization of the text, grammatical appropriateness, ability to provide appropriate information, etc.... The column also contains statistics on individual test scores, with averages and standard deviations, broken down by two distinct groups: Total Group and Standard Group.

The distinction between Total Group and Standard Group is a particularly significant and very useful for analysis. As is well known, U.S. schooling is particularly sensitive to the presence of native and heritage speakers. This presence can be particularly strong in certain contexts and for certain languages. Also, the College Board is particularly attentive to this situation, following the principles stated in the ACTFL *World Standards* from which it draws the theoretical framework for the AP exams. Indeed, as mentioned earlier, the Course Description explicitly states that specific syllabuses can be constructed for these students.

The specificity of native and heritage speakers is reflected in the ability to follow a specific syllabus and, consequently, also in the scores obtained on the exam. Therefore, it becomes particularly important to divide the analysis of the results of those who are native or heritage speakers from the others.

The College Board defines the Standard Group (SG) students as:

> students that generally receive most of their foreign language training in U.S. schools. They did not indicate on their answer sheet that they regularly speak or hear the foreign language of the exam, or that they lived for one month or more in a country where the language is spoken.

That is, the Standard Group includes all the students that are not native or heritage speakers or lived in a country where the language is spoken. The Standard Group identifies the students who study the foreign language only at school, in a formal educational context.

The percentage of students who report being native or heritage speakers varies greatly from language to language. See the Table 18, which does not include 2020:

	CHINESE	ITALIAN	SPANISH	FRENCH	GERMAN	JAPANESE
2018	73%	24%	67%	24%	31%	48%
2019	73%	25%	64%	24%	32%	50%
2021	74%	25%	66%	23%	29%	54%
2022	72%	27%	69%	25%	29%	56%

Table 18: Percentage of Native and Heritage Learners

The table shows that for some languages such as Spanish and Chinese the percentage is well above 60 percent. Chinese in some years reaches nearly 75 percent of students. For Japanese, about half of those taking the exam claim to be native or heritage speakers. While for languages such as Italian, French, and German, it ranges from an average of 25 percent for Italian and French to 30 percent for German.

The data regarding Italian seems to contradict those presented in the section where I discussed the profile of the Italian student. As we have seen, there seems to be a close relationship between Italian ancestry and the AP exam: the highest frequency of exams occurs in states where there is a higher presence of people claiming to be of Italian ancestry. In addition, some research seems to indicate that about 60 percent of Italian high school students claim to be of Italian ancestry (Dolci 2017 and references cited there). However, only less than 25 percent of students taking the AP exam claim to be native or heritage speakers. The contradiction is only apparent. As Census data show, while some 15 million Americans claim to be of Italian descent, only 500,000 claim to speak Italian at home. And the figure has been steadily declining since the year 2000. This may mean that the sense of Italian heritage seems to express itself no longer through language — especially in the younger generations — but through other manifestations, perhaps more related to the culture and image of Italy. It can therefore be said that the student of Italian, rather than being a heritage Italian language speaker, is a heritage Italian Culture "follower."[10]

The percentage distribution of scores — mean scores and standard deviation broken down by Total Group and Standard Group — is useful for the teacher, and it is also very useful for researchers and stakeholders. In fact, it provides a general overview of exam performance and any major or minor difficulties of individual FRQ tests.

However, the part that is most notable and important for the teacher and the researcher is the Chief Reader Report in which the Chief Reader analyzes the results obtained by all students on the various FRQ tests, identifying any weaknesses and, most importantly, giving teachers suggestions for improving student performance.

In what follows, I will first analyze the distribution of scores and then move on to analyze the reports written by the Chief Readers.

THE AP ITALIAN SCORES DISTRIBUTION

Scoring Statistics and the Score Distribution can provide teachers and especially researchers with some particularly interesting data on exam performance. In addition, the site provides access to statistics from many years back. This also makes it possible to conduct a particularly interesting longitudinal type of analysis.

Before moving on to the data analysis, it is imperative to remember that there were two different Course Descriptions in the period 2011-2022. One from 2011 to 2019 and the other from 2021 onward. This also resulted in a slight change in the first part of the exam, as we saw in the previous section. Since the 2021 exam, the session with multiple-choice questions has changed and is now the same as the other foreign languages. In addition, we should remember that the 2020 exam had a special procedure. With these caveats in mind, we find in the following chart the score means from 2012 to 2022.

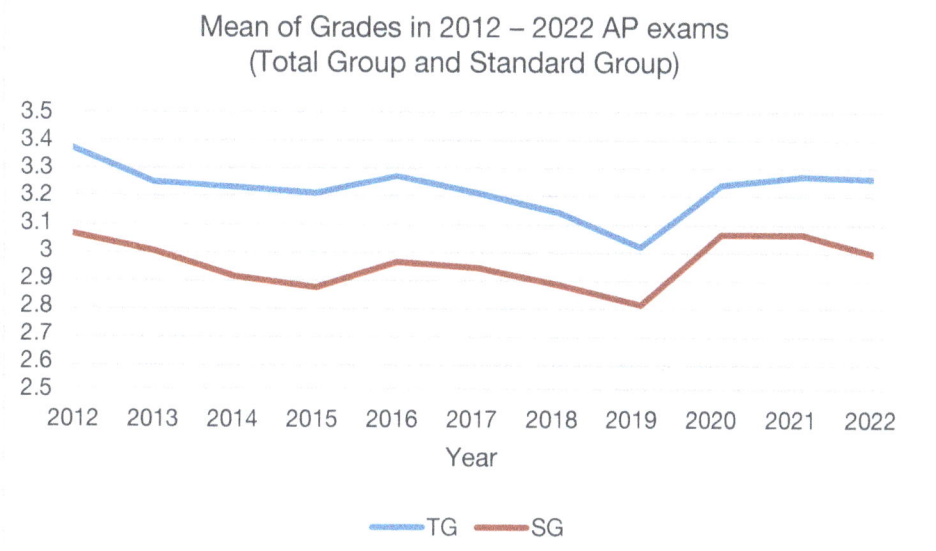

Chart 11: Mean of Grades in 2012 – 2022 AP exams

Chart 11 reports the averages of examinations held from 2012 to 2022 distinguishing the results of the Standard Group from those of the Total Group. As might be expected, the two groups follow the same trend, but the Standard Group average is always lower than that of the Total Group. In addition, the graph shows a constant decrease of the mean of degrees over the years until 2019, from 3.37 in 2012 to 3.02 in 2019, with 2016 representing the only exception.[11] In 2020, the exam average rises significantly. The figure surely depends on the type of exam that year, which was held in a reduced form due to the COVID emergency. The tests in 2021 and 2022 were as usual. It is intriguing that in 2021 and 2022 the mean rises again. It might depend on two factors: the adoption of the New Course Description and the slightly changed first part of the exam, the multiple-choice questions. However, we do not have any data that may or may not confirm this hypothesis. An analysis of the Standard Group's sole performance shows that, if the curve continues a downward trend, the mean even worsens until 2019. Chart 12 shows that over the 2012-2022 period the Standard group average was above the level 3 threshold only in 2012, 2013 and then in 2020 and 2021.

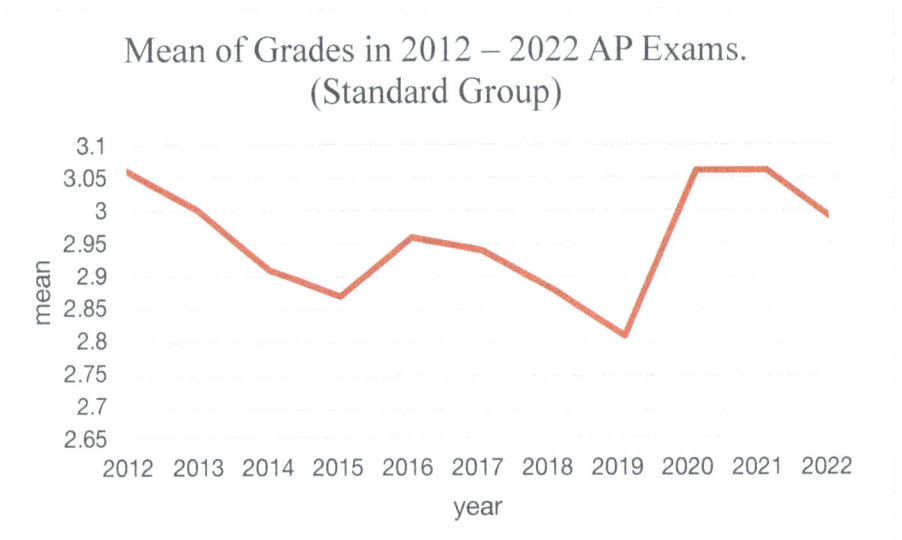

Chart 12: Mean of Grades in 2012 – 2022 AP Exams

The reason for the results below the overall Standard Group average is clear: the Group that represents 75 percent of all students excludes students who speak Italian at home and those who live in Italy, or spend a significant amount of time there, i.e., native speakers or heritage speakers. It therefore includes only students who learn Italian at school in a formal setting and who have no chance, except sporadically, to communicate in Italian outside the classroom.

These numbers (Chart 11 and 12) should be a reason for concern. In fact, the Total Group's average grade over the 2012-2022 period is only slightly above 3, which, according to the College Board, represents the basic level of qualification for college credits.[12]

However, from 2011 to 2022 the Standard Group's average grade is above 3 only in 2012 and 2013 and in 2020 and 2021. The Standard Group students who obtained a 3 or higher grade went from 68.5 percent in 2012 to 62 percent in 2019, rises to 72.2 percent in 2021 but fell to 65.8 percent in 2022. The Total Group went from 74.4 percent in 2012 to 70.5 percent in 2022.

An analysis of the trend for grades 3, 4, and 5 provides further proof of the general downward trend.

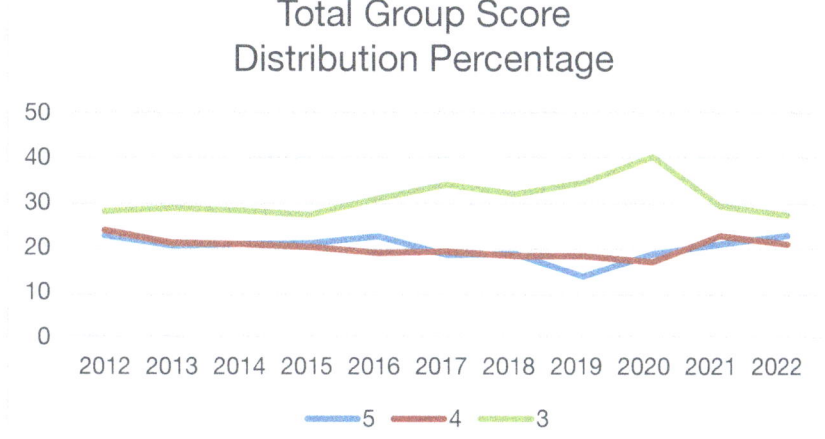

Chart 13: Grades 3-5 trend in 2012-2022. Total Group

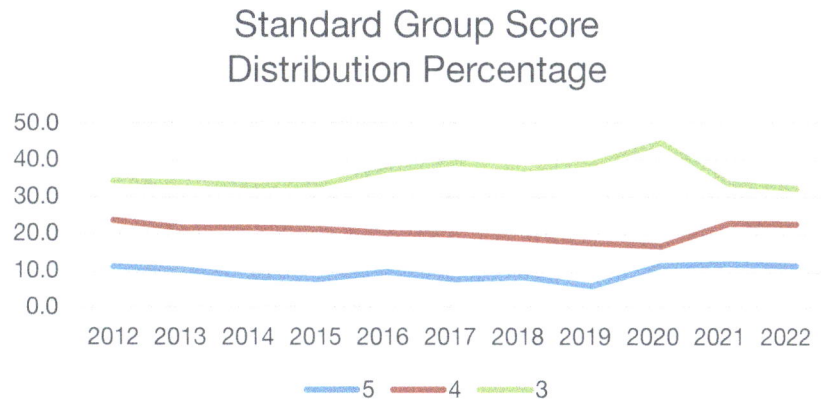

Chart 14: Grades 3-5 trend in 2012-2022. Standard Group

Charts 13 and 14 show that the percentage of the highest grades, 5 and 4, decrease over the years for both the Total and Standard Groups. In the Total Group, the 4s go from 23.7 percenter in 2012 to 18.1 percent in 2019, while the 5s go from 22.6 percent in 2012 to 13.6 percent in 2019. Within the Standard Group, the 4s go from 23.5 in 2012 to 17.4 in 2019, while the 5s are reduced by almost half: from 11 percent in 2012 to 5.8 percent in 2019. Consequently, in addition to the 3s, also the 2s and the 1s increase.

Over the same period, in the Total Group the 2s go from 19.5 to 24.6, while the 1s go from 6.1 percent to 9.3 percent in 2019. In the Standard Group the 2s go from 23.5 percent to 28.1 percent while the 1s go from 7.9 percent to 9.9 percent in 2019. Leaving apart 2020, for the reasons already explained, in 2021 and 2022, when the new Course Description is operating, we register a small increase of 4s and 5s and a significant decrease of 3s with respect to 2019. Therefore, during the period 2012-2022 almost one third of the students who took the Italian Language and Culture AP scored less than 3. The percentage rises to around 40 percent for the Standard Group.[13]

While it may not be of much comfort, it is noteworthy that the Italian Language and Culture exam results reflect to some degree those displayed by the other AP foreign languages Standard Groups, as we see in Chart 15:

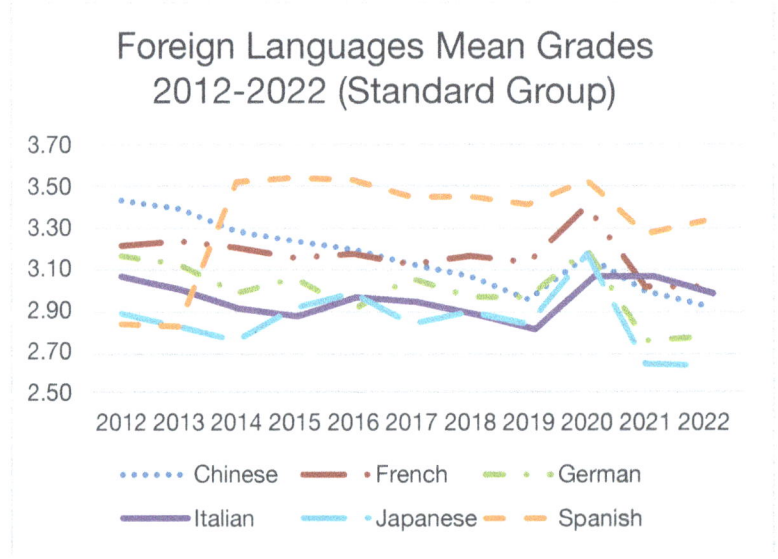

Chart 15: Foreign Language AP Mean grades Standard Group. 2012- 2022

All foreign languages exams in the Standard Group show an average decrease in scores from 2012 to 2022, apart from 2020 exam. Only Spanish with 3.3 and French with 3.1 are above the minimum in 2022.[14] The others are all below 3: Chinese with 2.92, German with 2.77, Japanese with 2.86 and Italian with 2.98. Chinese shows the worst decrease in the period 20112-2022, while the other Foreign Languages have the same behavior.

Italian shows the least decrease in 2021 and 2022 with respect to the other languages. If we analyze the Total Group score distribution, data change significantly. In fact, we should expect that Foreign Languages with a significant percentage of native and heritage students behave better than the others. This is exactly the case. In fact, the difference between the Standard Group and the Total Group is much more significant for Chinese and Spanish than the difference for German and Italian.

THE FREE RESPONSE QUESTIONS ANALYSIS

The first part of the AP exam, composed of multiple-choice questions, assesses interpretive communication, while the second aims to assess the student's productive and creative competence in foreign language. Specifically, the second part tests interpersonal and presentational competence in writing, speaking, and interacting. This part, because of its task types, is called Free-Response questions.

As we saw in the presentation, the Course Description of the AP program greatly emphasizes the development of the student's ability to use language creatively, according to the principles outlined by the ACTFL *World Readiness Standards*. For this reason, the College Board provides very detailed analyses of this second part of the exam. Which is also the subject of detailed scrutiny by the Chief Readers. We also want to underline, as the Chief Readers repeatedly do, that the analysis of this part of the exam provides very useful insights for teachers who should perhaps pay more attention to it. It can also provide significant data for scientific research and for proposing training courses to teachers that might more appropriately meet their needs.

For example, one might wonder if there is a difference in scores between the two parts of the exam, and, therefore, if the students perform better on one test than on the other and, also, if there are differences between the Standard Group score compared to the Total Group ones. And, finally, what are the most difficult tests for which students need to be better prepared. See Chart 16:

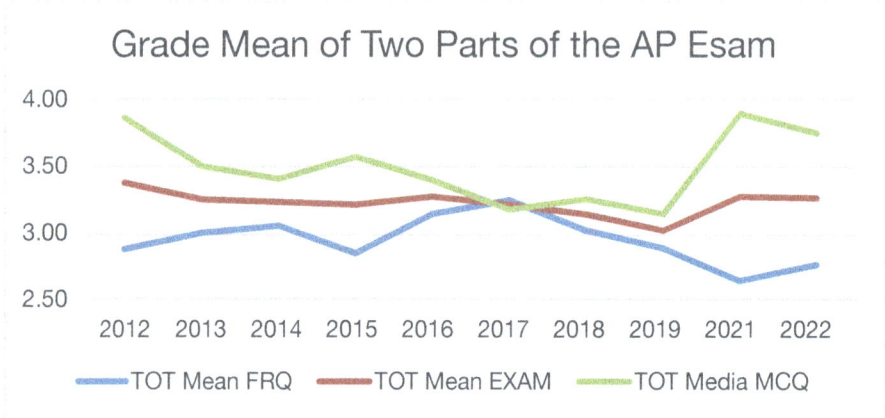

Chart 16: Mean comparison between the two parts of the exams

The graph shows that the first part of the exam the part that assesses the Interpretive communication, always has a higher average than the part that assesses the interpersonal and presentational writing and speaking, apart from the surprising figure in 2017. Interestingly, this difference is not always constant. The 2021 figure seems to be particularly significant. In fact, it represents the first rehearsal of the exam after the adoption of the new Course Description and the first time the new version of the first part of the exam is offered.

The figures shown in the graph provoke some further reflection. In particular, the competency in interpretive communication, measured in the MCQ section, has a virtually constant negative trend from 2012 to 2019 when it registers an average of 3.15. However, as I mentioned earlier, in 2021 the average is 3.89. A significant increase that persists in 2022 as well. In any case, the average of the MCQs always remains above 3. In contrast, the average of the FRQs, that is, of the second part of the exam, always remains below 3 apart from the period 2016-2018 when it also records the highest average of 3.24 in 2017, surprisingly surpassing the MCQs average. But after 2017, the average FRQ falls steadily, registering its lowest point precisely in 2021, the year of the first exam with the new Course Description. In 2022, however, there is a slight rise. Analysis of the graph also shows that there is no simultaneous increase in average MCQs and FRQs during the 2012-2022 period. The two components appear to have opposite behaviors. This trend is demonstrated by the analysis of the average total exam, which remains virtually constant over the period with values just above three, apart from 2019.

The behavior of the Standard Group is the same as that of the Total Group, as is to be expected, given that more than two-thirds of the students taking the AP Italian exam belong to this group. With one difference: the data gets worse.

The Standard Group shows an average of 2.94 over the 2012-2022 period and an average of 2.70 in the Free Response Questions, for the Standard Group, the average of the exam is above 3 only in 2012-2013, and in 2012, the average of the FRQ is always significantly below 3.

The year 2017 had a particular and, in some ways, unexpected behavior, since the average of the Free Response Questions exceeded the exam average in that year for both the Total Group and the Standard Group. In the latter, it even exceeded the threshold of 3.

Therefore, one can conclude that the students tend to find the second part of the exam more complicated than the first section. This difficulty is accentuated even more in the case of the Standard Group students, since, in general, they do not even reach the qualification threshold in the subject exam.

The reasons for such behavior are not easily detectable and are beyond the scope of this study. They certainly depend on many factors. One reason, as is well known to all teachers and well-studied by research in Second Language Acquisition, is that for a foreign language learner, productive competence, both oral and written, is certainly more difficult to develop than interpretive competence. This difficulty could be coupled with the more complicated procedure of the exam, which might create anxiety in the student and affect his or her performance. The College Board, as we have said, is particularly attentive to this part of the exam, which mirrors the importance given in the syllabus for the development of these skills. In fact, many of the sample activities offered in the Course Description, and in the teachers' part of the site focus on this aspect. The puzzling fact, which I will also emphasize better later, is that over the years, from 2012 to 2022, there has been no improvement in average scores, either in the exam in total or in the two tests, except in the MCQ test in 2021, with the new Course Description. In the same year, however, there is significant lowering of the FRQ test. A deeper analysis for possible causes could be an engaging and desirable avenue of research.

Having demonstrated that the second part of the exam is more complicated than the first, we can ask ourselves if there are differences in the score between the questions that form it. This second part consists of four different tests each assessing a specific competence.

1. E-mail replay, assessing Interpersonal writing
2. Persuasive essay (in 2019 Course Description it is named Argumentative essay), assessing Presentational Writing
3. Conversation, assessing Interpersonal speaking
4. Cultural comparison, assessing Presentational speaking.

Again, the College Board provides very detailed and in-depth data that allow for analysis.

For the specific review of the four tests, we will focus specifically on the behavior of the Standard Group. For two main reasons. The first because, as we have seen, the behavior of the Standard Group mirrors that of the totality of students, albeit with worse results. Moreover, the Standard Group student, not a native or heritage learner, is the typical student who attends Italian language classes, and learns the language only in the educational context.

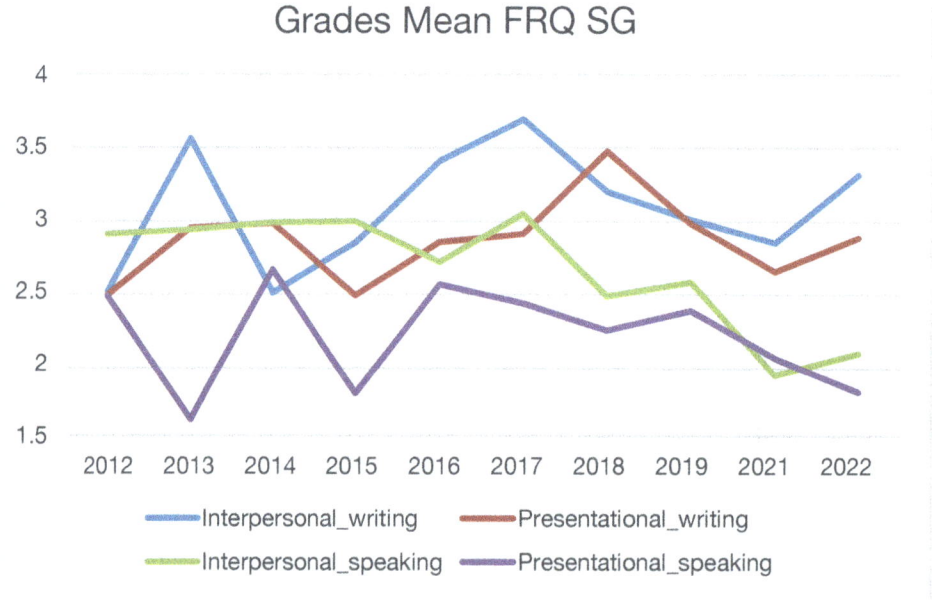

Chart 17: Standard Group grades mean in the four questions.

The Graph might look a bit complicated to read but some trends emerge clearly. All four modes show a fluctuating trend, which accentuates in some cases. The students' worst performances are in speaking. The "Presentational Speaking" (PS) Cultural Comparison task shows the lowest average in 2012-2022. The task requires that the student make a two-minute presentation in response to a prompt on a cultural topic. The score for this task fluctuates widely but remains below the average score of 2.5 (SG), with minimum levels of 1.63 in 2013, 1.81 in 2015, and 1.82 in 2022. The score for the Interpersonal Speaking task (IS), in which the student has "[t]o respond to questions as part of a simulated conversation," is more constant. The task average in the 2012-2022 period stands at 2.66 for SG, with a significant drop between 2017 and 2018. The "Interpersonal Writing" (IW) task consists of "reading and replying to an e-mail message," and shows the highest average over the period: 3.09 for SG. It is the only category that exceeds 3 on average. This task also shows a fluctuating trend, with a minimum of 2.51 in 2014 and a maximum of 3.69 in 2017. The "Presentational Writing" (PW) task, which requires "to write a persuasive (argumentative) essay," shows an average, over the same period, of 2.79 for Standard Group. The year 2018 shows the high score for both the Total Group and the Standard Group, whose 2017 score is the highest for the period.

In summary, we can say that the data again confirm what the specific literature has amply demonstrated and what all teachers have experienced in their daily practice. Among the Free Response Questions task, those who assess writing, both Interpersonal and Presentational, record better results than those who assess speaking. The Presentational Speaking (PS) mode turns out to be the most challenging test for the students, with a constant score below 3 for SG and slightly higher for TG.

We said above that the causes of such behavior are surely many, some more easily identifiable, others less obvious. In addition to those discussed above, for example, there could be the different weight and mode of evaluation of individual tests during correction; indeed, one aspect worth investigating. In the next section, I will propose an explanation for these phenomena by analyzing the Chief Readers' Reports.

THE CHIEF READERS' REPORTS

The AP Program consists of three basic moments that must be aligned with each other: the course framework, the preparation of the exam, and its correction. Expert committees composed of high school teachers, college faculty, representatives of institutions, etc. are appointed for these three moments. The first part of the exam, the part formed by MCQs, is corrected automatically. The second part of the exam is corrected by an expert panel consisting of specifically trained college faculty and AP course teachers, the AP Readers. The AP Readers are coordinated by a Chief Reader who monitors and ensures the quality of the correction process, its uniformity and correspondence to the set standards. After the exams have been corrected, the Chief Reader, writes a report in which he or she analyzes the students' answers.

The annual report written by the Chief Reader is beneficial to both teachers and researchers. It provides a detailed analysis of all four tasks related to the Free Response Questions and describe each task's aims and how the students responded. The Chief Reader analyzes the most frequent errors and, finally, proposes a series of recommendations and suggestions to teachers: for the details, researchers and teachers can refer directly to the College Board website reports. Here, we will analyze some specific points to understand if there have been similar issues over the years and if and how they have been addressed and eventually resolved.

The reports all have a similar structure. The first page of the report shows the number of readers who corrected the exams in that year and various statistics broken down by Total Group and Standard Group: namely, the number of corrected exams, the distribution of scores in absolute numbers and percentages, and the average. The Chief Reader then provides a detailed picture of each Free Response Questions task, its goals, and the results thereof, of the most common errors found. Finally, the Chief Reader offers advice and suggestions to the teacher for the future.

The ten reports analyzed here have been prepared by the following Chief Readers: Frank Nuessel (2012), Giuseppe Cavatorta (2013-2016), Paola Morgavi (2017-2019), and Federica Santini (2021-2022). The two last reports are based on the Course and Exam description released in 2019. Due to the completely changed structure of the 2020 exam, there is no Chief Raeder Report for the 2020 session published on the College AP website.

THE ANALYSIS OF THE FREE RESPONSE QUESTIONS

The four tests in the second part of the exam are supposed to measure the Interpersonal Writing Mode, the Presentational Writing Mode, the Interpersonal Speaking Mode, and the Presentational Speaking Mode. The four questions had the same weight, 12,5 percent each. Thus, the forum questions weighted 50 percent of the whole exam.

The first task assesses the student's Interpersonal Mode's writing skills by having them compose a reply to an e-mail message. The response was assessed on how well the student accomplished the task and received a general score. Students then had to demonstrate two integrated skills: first, understanding the text of the e-mail and then responding appropriately. The topics could vary. In 2019, for example, the topic was Famiglia e Società. The context was provided by an e-mail from a manager of an International Festival offering information about the program. Students were expected to answer why they were interested in attending the festival and their lodging preferences. In 2021 the topic was Famiglia Contemporanea. The context was an e-mail form a travel agency offering information about a trip in Italy. Students were expected to answer providing some details about their trip answering about how much they wanted to spend and about the services they needed.

This task shows the highest average result (3.28 for the Total Group and 3.09 for the Standard Group) over the 2012-2022 period, although inside a fluctuating trend. Almost the same typology of errors repeats itself in all reports and recommendations. From a pragmatic point of view, the major problem regards the appropriate register, as all the Chief Readers point out. Other linguistic errors are the "noticeable lack of idiomatic language" and the "lack of accuracy and control of grammar." Instead, the students could "maintain an appropriate exchange to the task," even "though many failed to seek additional information." The situation does not change much in 2021 and 2022. But while in 2021 the Standard Group does not average 3 points, in 2022 it averages 3.31, one of the highest among the ten years of exams analyzed. Even in 2021 and 2022, however, the Chief Reader points out that "several responses used an inappropriate register" and that "Some responses showed Spanish or English interference ("necesito," "lugare," "novio," "suggezione," "marveloso," ecc.).

The writing in the Presentational Communicative Mode task requires that students write an essay. Also, in this case the skills involved were integrated. Students had to rely on three sources of information: two written texts and one oral text. They then had 40 minutes to write their essay. Again, the assessment for this question was holistic and was based on the student's ability to know how to present and defend their opinion on the topic by demonstrating effective use of resources and analyzing different points of view.

In 2021, the topic was "Identità privata e Pubblica." Students had to "express their opinion about the importance of knowing the language of the country in which one lives in order to feel a sense of belonging to it" (Santini 2021, 5), while in 2022 the topic was Global Challenges (Sfide globali). Students had to write an essay about the importance of finding creative solutions to address pollution (Santini 2022, 5).

As for the previous one, the Chief Readers highlight that many of the students' errors are due to poor preparation. Here are some of their remarks: "Some students were not prepared to write a persuasive essay with clarity and accuracy"; "The presentational writing task may be unfamiliar to many students." They underscore the students' difficulties in organizing the structure of the essay, in understanding the resources and, consequently, in "address[ing] the prompt": "Some students did not demonstrate an understanding of the distinct points of view and the information contained in each of the sources."

All reports underline the lack of accuracy in using the language: "Lack of accuracy and variety in grammar, syntax and usage. [..] (2012-2022). Even of structures that should be well learned: There were also frequent errors in the subject-verb and noun-adjective agreements" (2012-2022). The Standard Group always scores below three, with the exception of 2018. In 2017, 2018, and 2019 there is a positive trend. Morgavi (2017, 2018, 2019) emphasizes how "[m]ost students were able to identify the main idea(s) of each source, some supporting details and the intent of the text." But students continued to make basic language errors: "[T]here was frequent use of verbs in the infinitive, indicating that many students struggle with tense recognition and conjugation" (2018). The years 2021 and 2022, with the new Course and Exam Description, show a decrease in scores. Especially in 2021 with a mean for the Standard Group of 2,65 Santini (2021) in her report underlines a "general lack of accuracy and variety in grammar, syntax and language use" and that "a very few responses demonstrated the ability to identify product and practices related to the topic and discern the perspectives behind them" (Santini 2021, 6).

The third task assesses speaking in the Interpersonal Mode. Students had to respond as if they were part of a simulated conversation. Students were expected to respond to five audio prompts on a familiar topic; they had to understand the prompt and answer accordingly.

In 2019 the topic was "Vita Contemporanea," and the prompt was about violence and dangers involved in sports. In 2022 the topic was "Families and Communities." Students needed to respond to "five prompts spoken by Enrico, an Italian friend who is hosting the student in his house and who wishes to discuss his group of friends and some possible plans for the night and the weekend" (Santini, 2022).

This task had the most consistent results over the years, with an average of 2.86. In 2018, however, there was a significant drop to 2.48 in the average grade for the Standard Group students (SG), while remaining as low as 2.57 in 2019. Furthermore, the Chief Readers underline a repetition of similar errors: "Lack of comprehensibility and clarity of expression," and "students did not use the appropriate register" are the most frequent comments, while the most common content errors depend on the fact that "[s]ome students did not provide appropriate information" and "some students did not provide an exchange appropriate to the task." In 2017 and 2018, most of the errors were concentrated in few questions. Although the communicative exchanges were "mostly uncomplicated," the students mainly "provided incorrect information" because they "did not understand some key words." In 2021 and 2022, the scores reach the worst result in ten years. In 2021 the mean is 1.94 for the Standard Group, while in 2022 the mean is 2022. Santini (2021) underlines that two questions were the most problematic. It was difficult for many students to "understand the questions, express their opinion and support it," due to misinterpretation/misunderstanding of vocabulary. In 2022 the mean is a bit higher, but still under three: 2.09. Santini (2022) writes that "the majority of responses demonstrated that the students understood the topic but did not always show an understanding of the specific meaning." Most students used basic vocabulary and "limited idiomatic language."

The fourth task assesses speaking in the Presentational Communicative Mode by having students make a comparative oral presentation on a cultural topic. Therefore, in addition to demonstrating linguistic-communicative skills, students must also show knowledge of the Italian culture, perhaps the critical topic in the AP Syllabus.

Students were allotted 4 minutes to read the topic and prepare the presentation and then 2 minutes to deliver the presentation. Chief Readers' reports underline that "the presentation had to compare the student's own community to an area of the Italian-speaking world, demonstrating understanding of cultural features of the Italian-speaking world."

For example, in 2019 and 2022 the topic was "Vita Contemporanea." In 2019 the cultural comparison was about the role of women in the labor market. In 2022 the task was about the role of open-air markets (food, clothes, etc.).

This task shows the most fluctuating results and constantly lowest scores, with an average of 2.25. In 2013 and 2015, the scores were even lower, below 2.00, whereas the highest point was reached in 2014 with 2.65, which overtook the Interpersonal Writing task. In 2021 and 2022, the trend is almost the same. But in 2021 this task scores a bit higher than Interpersonal Speaking, even though the mean is 2.05. In 2022 the mean is 1.82. One of the lowest, similar to 2013 and 2015.

Errors in pronunciation and intonation, specific to the task, coincide with the usual linguistic-communicative grammar, syntax, appropriateness, formal register errors, and difficulties in organizing the text. But these are not the areas that make the task particularly challenging for the students. The Chief Readers always emphasize how

> [s]tudents did not demonstrate a complete understanding of the Italian context to which they were comparing their own culture.
>
> Students did not provide a clear comparison of their community with that of the target culture [...].
>
> Responses were conducted in general terms and made no reference to any culture/community.

Students have often failed to grasp the close link between linguistic-communicative structures and cultural aspects, such as in 2015, when several students "misunderstood the prompt and, instead of talking about the importance of 'fare bella figura,'" they talked about the importance of "avere una bella figura"; or in 2018, when "[s]ome responses interpreted piazza as plaza (i.e., a shopping centre or strip mall) and concluded that there are no plazas in Italy." In 2019, the Chief Reader wrote that:

> [m]any responses showed stereotypical representations of women in the target culture and/or presented outdated content that does not reflect the role of women in contemporary Italian culture.

Also, in 2021 and 2022, Santini underlines that responses did not develop any comparison while discussing the topic within the target culture or their own culture. Also, "a few responses did not address the prompt and talked instead about subjects irrelevant to the topic."

THE CHIEF READERS' RECOMMENDATIONS

To avoid making the same mistakes, the Chief Readers have drawn up a series of tips for teachers to "help them improve the performance of their students." The Chief Readers are sometimes surprised by the types of errors found, such as those of the linguistic-communicative type, affecting structures that should have been fully assimilated. A Chief Reader notes that "[s]tudents had to maintain mostly uncomplicated communicative exchanges." Notwithstanding what preceded, some students failed the item. The Chief Readers reiterate constantly that students need to "[p]ay attention to grammar and syntax," and advise teachers that "the almost exclusive use of Italian in class should be adopted from level 1 on."

More frequently, however, the errors found are traced back to the students' lack of practice in performing a specific task. Consequently, the Chief Readers always advise that the teachers allow the students to practice during the course, not only on the particular task but indeed under the same conditions. Students need training with mock tasks and realistic exam simulations. For example, for the Interpersonal Communicative Writing task, where the students must write an e-mail, here is what the Chief Reader wrote in 2012:

> Students are already accustomed to responding to e-mails, but most of these involve interpersonal writing with friends in which the familiar register is used. This task, however, required the use of the formal register.

Consequently, the suggestion for teachers was to "[g]uide students through the task's instructions and ensure that they know all its requirements" and "[p]repare simulated e-mail reply writing tasks for periodic practice under actual exam conditions, and score these practice responses using the scoring guidelines."

Almost every year the Chief Readers repeat the same advice, often verbatim. Also, in 2021 Santini once more advises teachers to "help students familiarize themselves with the task." Again, she suggests to teachers to urge students "to use the sample e-mail tasks available on AP classroom, in the AP Daily videos and in previous AP exams."

For the second task, one of the most common recommendations is "practice in writing essays in which they have to refer to three separate sources, as in the exam." Morgavi (2019) and Santini (2022) advise teachers to "make sure students understand the nature and characteristics of and argumentative (in 2019 persuasive) essay. Both Chief Readers underline, as well, the need to "provide students with strategies on how to express their own viewpoint on a topic." For the third task, "students need to practice listening to a wide variety of male and female voices," as in the exam; for the fourth task, "students [should be provided] with templates for this task to use them in the year to build their skills in organizing and comparing information."

Many errors the students make are due to the lack of familiarity with exam content and exam modalities. The Chief Readers underline the need to "instruct students to read and follow the directions very carefully"; to "[g]uide students through the tasks' instructions and ensure that they know and understand all its requirements"; to "help students become familiar with the equipment to be used during the administration of the actual exam"; and, "teachers should also train their students to optimize the time they have (four minutes) for carefully reading the prompt." It is also significant for the Chief Readers to "[e]xplain the scoring guidelines for the task to students to familiarize them with the expectations for performance," and so on.

Other suggestions are more methodological and related to the syllabus: "[E]xpose students to as many authentic materials as possible"; "provide models of comparison between one's home community and the target culture"; "[Students] are expected to be able to go beyond 'product' and 'practices' and relate these two aspects to socio-cultural 'perspectives'"; "provide students with strategies for how to express their own view point on a topic and build their argument"; "in class, present and discuss cultural material in the target language"; "have students practice informal, spontaneous conversation in class"; "students need to engage in activities that promote the ability to respond to dialogic situations in a natural and appropriate fashion in line with the give-and-take of a speech event," and so on.

Such methodological and content-related suggestions from the Chief Readers are a precious resource for the AP instructors based on what they can modify their teaching habits. As is well known, schools and teachers who want to offer an AP course must follow a well-defined procedure established by the College Board. The key moment of this process is the AP Course Audit, during which experts analyze and evaluate the syllabus proposed by the school. The College Board "provide[s] teachers and administrators with clear guidelines on curricular and resource requirements for AP course" (2020: 1), and it reaffirms its unequivocal support for the principle according to which each school should develop and implement its own curriculum, although an AP course must comply with the guidelines provided to receive the approval. The College Board stresses the close connection between the AP course and the AP exam. The course and the exam share the same theoretical principles and the same linguistic-communicative and cultural goals. "The AP Test Development Committees are responsible for developing each AP Exam, ensuring the exam questions are aligned to the course framework" (2020, 2). Although the College Board has prepared all these tools and continuously controls the courses and the examinations, the analysis of the Chief Readers' reports shows that there is still much to do. The Chief Readers' recommendations and comments show a "breach" between the Free Responses Questions and the AP Course syllabus.[15]

The interrelation between a course and a test, and its influence on the teacher's course syllabus, have been much studied by scientific literature and has been labeled the "washback effect" (Wall and Alderson 1993; Bailey 1999; Cheng and Watanabe 2004).[16] This expression indicates the effect that a test and its structure can have on teaching and the syllabus. It might impact determining the course goals, which will be matched with those of the test. For example, if a test is primarily designed to assess grammar competence, this would become the course's main objective and, therefore, influence the choice of materials. Then, still as an example, if the test only uses written texts, or such texts are exclusively focused on a specific subject, the teacher will mainly use the same typology.

Finally, the pushback effect influences the methodology adopted, with the teachers proposing only exercises that simulate the exam, e.g., using mainly multiple choices, short answers, etc. From this overly simplified description, it appears clear that the washback effect may often receive unfavorable consideration. As in the example given, it can severely limit a harmonious and well-balanced development of all the linguistic and communicative skills by only focusing on those assessed in the test. The student focuses on "passing the exam" rather than learning the language. However, it can also have a positive effect — e.g., in helping to write syllabuses that conform to standards — thus stimulating innovation and curriculum updating. It can also encourage both teachers and students to continually reflect on their teaching practice and their own learning experience, respectively.[17] As Alderson says: "[…] it is at least as much the teacher who brings about washback, be it positive or negative, as it is the test" (2004, X). We could also add families, the institution, and the students themselves.

The pushback effect might also be at work in the AP Program. The AP exam might have an impact on the AP Course either negatively or positively. There are many factors and actors at work on this regard. However, the AP Program is a rather different case: in fact, the College Board defines the AP as a program in which the course and the exam (not the test) are two components of the same system and not two separate elements developed by two different entities.[18]

The AP Program main goal isn't just to earn college credits. It has a strong educational goal "Through AP courses in 38 subjects, each culminating in a challenging exam, students learn to think critically, construct solid arguments, and see many sides of an issue — skills that prepare them for college and beyond" (*AP Course description*, 2020, 1).

In brief, the AP Course and the AP exam are components of a single project, designed by a group of experts who are "responsible for drawing clear and well-articulated connections between the AP course and AP exam." (2011, 2). They share the same theoretical framework defined by the *Standards for Foreign Language Learning in the 21st Century*, which are linked to the *ACTFL Performance Guidelines* (2011, 4). Thus, the exam assesses the students' proficiencies in the Interpersonal, Interpretive and

Presentational modes of communication, as defined in both the *ACTFL Standards* and the *Performance Guidelines*. The AP Audit, as explained in the AP Course description, guarantees the connection between the curriculum and the exam (2011, 34-35).

The entire system is thus very coherent and does not allow for gaps between course and exam. Hopefully, the AP Program can stimulate a positive washback effect in the concept of a continuous language-education structure from K to 12 up to 16, by encouraging the creation of a vertical curriculum within a shared and cohesive theoretical and epistemological framework. Doing so can only enhance the harmonious development of the linguistic-communicative and cultural competencies in Italian language and culture without useless repetitions or omissions.[19]

Another aspect that emerges from the Chief Readers' reports confirms a possible gap between the course and the exam. Very often, the Chief Readers report the same types of errors made by most students, such as "many students did not develop […]"; "[…] unfamiliar to many students"; "there was abundant confusion"; "many essays lacked […]"; "there was a noticeable lack […]"; "several students misunderstood the prompt […]"; "it was hard for many students to accomplish the task"; "[o]ften students used inappropriate register"; and so on. Moreover, sometimes "practically none of the students correctly interpreted an important statement," or, "there was a misunderstanding of a key point."

The scores of the exam reflect these generalized errors. We already saw that from 2012 to 2018, the Free Response Questions totaled, on average, a lower score compared to the multiple-choice questions (only in 2017 did the average of FRQ exceed the threshold of 3, with 3.02). Over the same period, the sole task that, on average exceeded the threshold of 3, was Interpersonal Writing, with 3.11. All the others show scores below 3. Presentational Speaking shows the lowest average over the same period, i.e., 2.25. Additionally, the Standard Deviation is very low for all the tasks, which shows a general downward levelling on the grade scale, as testified by the low percentage of 5 and 4 grades. The new course description effective in 2019, but impacting the examination from 2021 onward, does not seem to have modified the situation to a notable extent.

These data suggest that the students' low performance might be due to insufficient rehearsal with mock exam tasks and an inadequate balance between the course goals and the level of performance required by the exam. Simply put, some of the tasks contained in the second part of the exam may be too challenging for the students.

There is no scientifically proven answer to such imbalance with the current data available: only speculation is possible. Hence, the following issues might be considered as potential topics for future research:

- The Course Audit may not be entirely accurate due to a possible disconnection between the curriculum content and the classroom activities.
- Perhaps it depends on an exam not well-calibrated with the course content or curriculum. It might be a teacher training issue if, for example, s/he finds some difficulties putting the syllabus into practice.
- Another reason might be a possible gap between the theoretical framework and the daily practice.
- Perhaps some teachers do not take full advantage of the resources made available by the College Board and other institutions.

A combination of all or some of the above points is also possible. Then, another reason could be the control over the selection of students allowed to enroll in the AP Program. Should students who do not possess an adequate level of competence to attend an AP Course be allowed to "try" the exam; their lack of competence would inevitably be reflected in the examination results. In other words, if, on the one hand, enrolling as many students as possible ensures that a good number of exams is taken, on the other hand the grade average can only be low. This gives rise to another issue, that is, if the decision to admit the students in the AP courses rests with the teacher or whether it is part of a broader strategy.

The above questions can be answered by collecting significant data through an Action-Research methodology that also involves colleges and universities. In fact, although the College Board already provides a large quantity of data and information, the community of teachers, experts, and institutions should complement such an effort by promoting the development of comprehensive and organic studies to collect the necessary data for subsequent analysis.

There are also broader actions possible involving all the stakeholders in a shared effort covering the short, medium, and long terms. The first and most important aspect is the continued, professional development of Italian teachers, both prospective and in-service, to guarantee constant updating, which is not limited to the AP Program but exploits its potential. Secondly, it is necessary to act in a unified and coordinated fashion to promote more effectively Italian language teaching.

CONCLUSIONS

To be sure, the history of the AP Italian Program is a success story. But it is also very fragile. With such small numbers, even a small crisis can have very serious consequences. The analysis I have done demonstrates that both quantitative and qualitative interventions are needed in order to ensure improvement. These two aspects are closely related. Therefore, it is necessary to reflect collectively in order to find the best strategies to increase the numbers. There are several possible strategies: The first is through the involvement of those who feel a cultural connection with Italy and its culture. We know very well that image of Italy enjoys high prestige that is linked to its cultural products, from fashion to economy, landscape, tourism, food, and its millennial culture. It is important to tie these aspects together with the knowledge of the Italian language as well; a goal here to communicate effectively the message that Italian culture can be more greatly appreciated if one knows the language.

We have seen that there is still much room for improvement in this regard, especially among people of Italian descent. In some contexts, the ratio of Italian language learners to Americans of Italian descent can surely be raised. A modest increase of said correlation would be notably advantageous to the above-mentioned language-education structure from K to 12 up to 16 as well as to the AP Italian Language and Culture Program, bringing it out of the danger zone and unto a more secure threshold. Another intervention strategy certainly originates from the promotion of studying Italian language and culture among Latinx students. Again, an effective strategy in these areas could lead to an increase in numbers that, in some contexts, are significant already. But one should not limit oneself to these only. The linguistic proximity between Spanish and Italian can also be used to convince those who study Spanish not as a heritage language. Thus, in a multilingual and intercomprehension linguistic perspective can and should involve all neo-Latin languages, including French.

One can also begin to think about whether to change the way the exam is delivered. We have seen that Chinese and Japanese students seem to benefit, albeit in different forms, from an online administration of the exam. Perhaps some thought might be dedicated to this possibility, to evaluate the potential benefit from an online format.

These strategies must necessarily be coupled to improvements in teaching as well, more professional development programming in this regard. From this perspective, then, the AP Program can be seen as an opportunity to create a virtuous circle that can only benefit the teaching and learning process of Italian at all levels, from K to 12 and beyond.

Once again, research — through accurate data collection followed by effective data analysis — can provide the grounds by which to build effective intervention tools. This current discussion, as I conclude for the time being, though seemingly fragmentary and inconclusive, will have achieved its purpose, if it stimulates other scholars to produce other, certainly more extensive work. The future of the AP Program and of the teaching of Italian in the USA surely depend on such an approach.

NOTES

[1] AP Italian Language and Culture Course and Exam Description (2020, 7).

[2] As we have seen, all schools offering AP courses have passed the AP Course Audit and are listed in the AP Course Ledger.

[3] https://apcentral.collegeboard.org/courses/ap-italian-language-and-culture/course-audit.

[4] https://apcentral.collegeboard.org/courses/ap-italian-language-and-culture?course=ap-italian-language-and-culture. Accessed November 2021.

[5] According to the Princeton Review, a 4 or a 5 is the AP score that will most likely earn college AP credit. https://www.princetonreview.com/college-advice/ap-scores. Retrieved November 2019.

[6] The accurate description is given in the 2011 Course description, pages 36-37.

[7] Section II – free response questions, will be analyzed in chapter 3.

[8] https://apstudents.collegeboard.org/courses/ap-italian-language-and-culture/assessment.

[9] https://apcentral.collegeboard.org/courses/ap-italian-language-and-culture/exam.

[10] Piero Bassetti identifies such a person as an "Italic." By Italic, he means a person who may or may not be of Italian descent but still has a cultural connection to what Italy represents. One could also speak in this case of cultural and not linguistic "Italianità" (Bassetti 2017).

[11] That is, close to 3, that is the minimum passing rate.

[12] I will look for an explanation for the decrease in the average of the scores from 2012 to 2019 in the next paragraph, through the words of the Chief Readers.

[13] The great majority of these students were enrolled in an AP course before taking the exam. The data on the Standard Group and the Total Group provided by the College Board are not divided by country. However, since U.S. students represent about 95 percent of the total, we can conclude that U.S. students and the Total Group share similar data.

[14] Spanish data of 2012 and 2013 look too low with respect to all the other years. We do not have an answer for this trend.

[15] It would be interesting to analyze also the first part of the exam with the multiple-choice questions. The evaluation of the students' behavior would add data to verify the hypothesis.

[16] See also Gifford and O'Connor (1992), and reference cited there for a discussion about this theme.

[17] For an in-depth discussion of the washback effect, see Cheng, Watanabe, and Curtis (2004).

[18] This is differently from the relationship between the TOEFL and an English language course. Notably, the director of NIE affirms that it might have a positive washback effect on school instruction and curricula (Maiellaro 2019, 11).

[19] Another aspect that needs specific analysis regards the textbooks that teachers and students use. Are authors aware of the specific AP syllabus? Do they include it in their textbooks?

Bibliography

College Board Websites

https://research.collegeboard.org/programs/ap

https://apcentral.collegeboard.org/courses/ap-italian-language-and-culture?course=ap-italian-language-and-culture

https://apcentral.collegeboard.org/courses/ap-italian-language-and-culture/exam

https://apcentral.collegeboard.org/courses/ap-italian-language-and-culture/exam/past-exam-questions?course=ap-italian-language-and-culture

https://apcentral.collegeboard.org/courses/ap-course-audit/about

https://apcourseaudit.inflexion.org/ledger/search.php

Works Cited

American Councils for International Education (ACIE). 2017. *The National K-12 Foreign Language Enrollment Survey Report*. ACIE, www.americancouncils.org. Retrieved June 2020.

American Council of Teachers of Foreign Language (ACTFL). 2002. *Foreign Language Enrollments in Public Secondary Schools, Fall 2000*. Alexandria: ACTFL.

American Council of Teachers of Foreign Language (ACTFL). 2008. *Foreign Language Enrollments in K–12 Public Schools: Are Students Prepared for a Global Society?* Alexandria: ACTFL.

Alderson, J. C. 2004. "Foreword." In *Washback in Language Testing*. Cheng, Liying, Yoshinori Watanabe, and Andy Curtis, eds. London: Lawrence Erlbaum Associates.

Angiolillo, P. F. 1966. "AATI Newletter." *Italica* 43.3: 323-332.

Angiolillo, P. F. 1967. "AATI Newsletter." *Italica* 44.2: 254-262.

College Board. 2011. *AP Italian Language and Culture. Course and Exam Description.* https://apcentral.collegeboard. org/media/pdf/ap-italian-language-and-culture-course-and-exam-description.pdf. Retrieved October 2018.

College Board. 2020. *AP Italian Language and Culture. Course and Exam Description.* https://apcentral.collegeboard. org/media/pdf/ap-italian-language-and-culture-course-and-exam-description.pdf, Retrieved July 2022.

Bailey, K. M. 1999. *Washback in Language Testing*. Ed. TOEFL Monograph MS 15 Series. Educational Testing Service ETS.

Baldelli, I., ed. 1987. *La lingua italiana nel mondo. Indagine sulle motivazioni allo studio dell'italiano*. Rome: Istituto dell'Enciclopedia Italiana.

Bancheri, S. 2010. "AP Italian Update" *AATI Newsletter* (Spring): 4.

Bancheri, S. 2017. "AATI National Italian Examination Results." *AATI Newsletter* (Fall): 19-20.

Bancheri, S. 2018. "AATI National Italian Examination Report." *AATI Newsletter* (Fall): 11-13.

Barker, D. G. 1967. "The History of Entrance Examinations." *Improving College and University Teaching* 15.4: 250-253.

Bassetti, P. 2017. *Let's Wake Up, Italics!* New York: John D. Calandra Italian American Institute.

Bigelow, D. N. and Lyman H. L. 1964. *NDEA. Languages and Area Centers. A report on the First 5 Years*. Washington, D.C.: US Department of Health, Education and Welfare.

Boorstin, D. J. 1973. *The Americans: The Democratic Experience*. New York: Random House.

Brinsmade, C. 1928. "Concerning the College Board Examinations in Modern Languages." *The Modern Language Journal* 13.2: 87-100.

Brinsmade, C. 1928. "Concerning the College Board Examinations in Modern Languages." *The Modern Language Journal* 13.3: 212-227.

Brown, H. D. and Priyanvada A. 2004. *Language Assessment: Principles and Classroom Practices*. White Plains: Pearson Education ESL.

Buchanan, M., A. 1926. "Italian Achievement Tests." *Italica* 3.2: 34-35.

Butler, K., D. 2001. "Defining Diaspora, Refining a Discourse." *Diaspora: A Journal of Transnational Studies* 10.2: 189-219.

Castiglione, P. B. 1959. "A Discussion: The Teaching of Italian and Its Problems." *Italica* 36.4: 287-290.

Cavatorta, G. 2013. "Student Performance Q&A: 2013 AP Italian Language Free-Response Questions." College Board. https://secure-media.collegeboard.org/ digitalServices /pdf/ap/apcentral/ap13_italian_language_qa.pdf. Retrieved July 2018.

Cavatorta, G. 2013. "AP Italian Language and Culture Exam 2013" *AATI Newsletter* (Fall): 8.

Cavatorta, G. 2014. "Student Performance Q&A: 2014 AP Italian Language and Culture Free-Response Questions" College Board. https:secure-media.collegeboard.org/ digitalServices/pdf/ap/apcentral/ap14-italian-language-qa.pdf. Retrieved July 2018.

Cavatorta, G. 2014. "AP Italian Language and Culture Results 2014" *AATI Newsletter* (Fall): 9.

Cavatorta, G. 2015. "Student Performance Q&A: 2015 AP Italian Language and Culture Free-Response Questions", College Board, 2015, https://secure-media.collegeboard. org/digitalServices/pdf/ap/ap15-italian-student-performance-qa.pdf. Retrieved July 2018.

Cavatorta, G. 2016. "Student Performance Q&A: 2016 AP Italian Language and Culture Free-Response Questions", College Board, https://secure-media.collegeboard.org/ digitalServices /pdf/ap/ap16_italian_lang_student_performance_qa.pdf. Retrieved July 2018.

Cavatorta, G. 2018. "Innovation and Increasing Enrollments in Italian Language Programs. Una sfida all'insegna dell'incertezza." *TILCA Special Issue: Innovation in Italian Programs and Pedagogy*. http://tilca.qc.cuny.edu/wp-content/uploads/2018 /TILCA%20 2018%20Special%20Issue.pdf. Retrieved October 2019

Cavatorta, G. 2019. "President's message" *AATI Newsletter* (Spring): 1-3.

Cavatorta, G. 2019. "President's Message"AATI *AATI Newsletter* (Fall): 1-3.

Commission on the Future of the APP, (2001)"Access to Excellence." New York: College Board. https://files.eric.ed.gov/fulltext /ED561056.pdf. Retrieved July 2018.

Challenge Success. 2013. "The Advanced Placement Program: Living Up To Its Promise?" 2013. Challenge Access, https://challengesuccess.org/wp-content/uploads/2021/ 04/ChallengeSuccess-AdvancedPlacement-WP.pdf. Retrieved July 2018.

Cheng, C & Watanabe, Y. with Curtis A. (eds). 2004. *Washback in Langnuage testing: Research, Context and Methods*. Mahwah, NJ: Lawrence Earlbaum Associates.

Cordasco, F. 1975. *The Italian Community and its Language in the United States The Annual Reports of the Italian Teachers Association*. Totowa: Rowman and Littlefield.

De Mauro, T., Vedovelli, M., Barni, M., Miraglia, L., eds. 2002. *Italiano 2000. I pubblici e le motivazioni dell'italiano diffuso fra stranieri*. Rome: Bulzoni.

Dennis, L., Lusin, N. 2018. "Enrollments in Languages Other Than English in United States Institutions of Higher Education, Summer 2016 and Fall 2016: Preliminary Report" Modern Language Association of America (MLA) Web Publication,https://www.mla.org/content/download/83540/file/2016-Enrollments-Short-Report.pdf. Retrieved October 2019.

Dolci, R., and Tamburri, A. J., eds. 2015. *Intercomprehension and Plurilingualism*. New York: John D. Calandra Italian American Institute, CUNY.

Dolci, R., 2017. "Profilo dello studente di lingua italiana nelle scuole USA." Noli, V. and A. Masi, (eds) *Annuario della Società Dante Alighieri*. Rome: Società Dante Alighieri: 219: 240

Dolci, R. 2018. *Il Giornalino di Prezzolini*. Florence: Franco Cesati Editore.

Educational Research Service. 1981. *Testing for College Admissions:Trends and Issues*. Arlington, VA: ETS.

Epstein, M. 1999. Thought about an AP-Type exam in Italian, AATI *Newsletter* (Fall 1999): 9.

Falbo, E. S. 1961. "FL Newsletter." *Italica* 38.2: 174-178.

Falbo, E. S. 1962. "FL Newsletter." *Italica* 39.3: 232-237.

Falbo, E. S. 1963. "AATI Newsletter." *Italica* 40.2: 198-206.

Falbo, E. S. 1964. "AATI Newsletter." *Italica* 41.2. 217-225.

Falbo, E. S. 1967. "Annual Meeting of the American Association of Teachers of Italian (1966)." *Italica* 44.1: 111-116.

Falbo, E. S. 1968. "Annual Meeting of the American Association of Teachers of Italian (1967)." *Italica* 45.1: 123-129.

Flattau, P. E. 2006. *The National Defense Education Act of 1958: Selected Outcomes*. Washington DC: Institute for Defense Analysis Science & Technology Policy Institute.

Fucilla, J. G. 1947. "Editorial Comment." *Italica* 24.4: 362-363.

Fucilla, J. G. 1967. *The Teaching of Italian in the United States*. New Brunswick: American Association of Teachers of Italian.

Fuess, C. M. 1950. *The College Board. Its First Fifty Years*. New York: Columbia University Press.

Gifford, B. R. and M. C. O' Connor (eds). 1992. *Changing Assessment*, New York: Springer.

Giordano, P. 2000. "AATI 1999 General Business Meeting." *Italica* 77.1: 143-150.

Giordano, P. 2001. "AATI 2000 General Business Meeting." *Italica* 78.1: 137-144.

Giovanardi, C., Trifone, P. 2012. *L'italiano nel mondo*. Rome: Carocci.

Goldberg, D., D. Looney and N. Lusin. 2015. *Enrollments in Languages Other Than English in United States Institutions of Higher Education, Fall 2013*. MLA Web Publication. 2015. https://www.mla.org/content/download/31180/file/EMB_enrllmnts_non Engl_2013.pdf. Retrieved July 2018

Golden, H. H. 1959. "FL Newsletter." *Italica* 36.2: 151-153.

Golden, H., H. 1960. "FL Newsletter." *Italica* 37.2: 158-161.

Golden, H. H. 1961. "Annual Meeting of the American Association of Teachers of Italian (1960)." *Italica* 38.1: 87-90.

Golden, H. H. 1962. "Annual Meeting of the American Association of Teachers of Italian (1961)." *Italica* 39.1: 85-86.

Golden, H. H. 1962. "The Teaching of Italian: The 1962 Balance Sheet." *Italica* 39.4: 276-288.

Haller, H. 2016. "Per una politica dell'italiano negli USA: alcune riflessioni." Librandi, R. and Piro, R., eds. *L'italiano della politica e la politica per l'italiano*. Florence: Franco Cesati Editore.

Hanson, F. A. 1992. *Testing Testing. Social Consequences of the Examined Life*. Berkeley: University of California Press.

Jamison, E. 2015. "1890-1969—Early History of the Advanced Placement Program: an Argument for Reform of the AP Language & Composition Exam." https://scholarworks.gsu.edu/englishdiss/137. Retrieved July 2018.

Jaschik, S. 2020. "College Board Says AP Testing a Success", https://www.insidehighered.com/admissions/article/2020/05/26/college-board-says-ap-testing-was-success-sued. Visited July 2021.

Jaschik, S. 2020. "Frustrations with AP Testing" https://www.insidehighered.com/admissions/article/2020/05/18/students-complain-they-cannot-submit-ap-tests. Visited July 2021.

Kleinhenz, C. 1999. "Questionnaire/survey for Italian Placement Examination", AATI *Newsletter* (Spring 1999): 8-9.

Kleinhenz, C. 1999. "President's Column", *AATI Newsletter*, (Fall 1999): 1-24.

Kibler, L. 1990. "Annual Meeting of the American Association of Teachers of Italian (1989)." *Italica* 67.1: 98-106.

Kibler, L. 1993. "Annual Meeting of the American Association of Teachers of Italian (1992)." *Italica* 70.2: 291-297.

Laggini, J. 1971. "Annual Meeting of the American Association of Teachers of Italian (1970)." *Italica* 48.1: 119-124.

Laggini, J. 1973. "Annual Meeting of the American Association of Teachers of Italian (1972)." *Italica* 50.1: 128-133

Laggini, J. E. 1974. "Annual Meeting of the American Association of Teachers of Italian (1973)." *Italica* 51.1: 100-104.

Lanza, I. L. 2009. Re-instating the AP Italian exam, *AATI Newsletter*, (Spring 2009): 6.

Lawrence, I., M., Rigol G., Van Essen, T., Jackson, C. A. 2003. *A Historical Perspective on the Content of SAT. College Board Research Report 2003-3*. New York: College Board.

Lebano, E. A. 1999. *Survey on the Italian Language in the U.S.A.* Welland, Ontario: Soleil.

Librandi, R., Piro, R., eds. 2015. *L'italiano della politica e la politica per l'italiano*. Florence: Franco Cesati Editore.

Liekar, C. Y. 2012. "The Advanced Placement Program in Pennsylvania: implications for Policies and Practice in K-12 and Higher Education." Doctor od Education Dissertation, University of Pennsylvania.

Looney, D. and N. Lusin. 2019. "Enrollments in Languages Other Than English in United States Institutions of Higher Education, Summer 2016 and Fall 2016 Report." MLA Web Publication. https://www.mla.org/content/download/147768/file/2016_Community_Colleges_Enrollment_Report_Revised.pdf. Retrieved October 2020.

Lucas, C. J. 2006. *American Higher Education, an history*. New York: Palgrave Mc Millan.

Ministero Affari Esteri e della Cooperazione Internazionale, (MAECI). 2016. *Stati Generali della lingau italiana nel mondo*. Rome: MAECI.

Ministero Affari Esteri e della Cooperazione Internazionale (MAECI). 2017. *L'Italiano nel mondo che cambia*. Rome: MAECI.

Ministero Affari Esteri e della Cooperazione Internazionale (MAECI). 2019. *L'Italiano nel mondo che cambia*. Rome: MAECI.

Maiellaro, G. 2019. "National Italian Exam", *AATI Newsletter* (Fall 2019): 11.

Maiellaro, G., Lubrano, M. J. 2019. "2019 AATI National Italian Examination Report." *AATI Newsletter* (Spring): 10.

Mancini, A. 2006. "Messaggio del presidente." *AATI Newsletter* (Fall 2006): 1-5.

Mattern, K. D., Show, E. J. and Xiong X. 2009. "The Relationship Between AP Exam Performance and College Outcomes. Research Report 2009-4." New York: College Board.

Mita, D. 2002. "Italian Language Advanced Placement Program." *AATI Newsletter* (Spring): 4-5.

Mollica, A. 1988. "Annual Meeting of the American Association of Teachers of Italian (1986, 1987)." *Italica* 65.1: 53-64.

Mollica, A. 1986. "Annual Meeting of the American Association of Teachers of Italian (1985)." *Italica* 63.4: 428-435.

Morgan, R. and Klaric, J. 2007. *AP Students in College: An Analysis of Five-Year Academic Careers*, New York: College Board. https://files.eric.ed.gov/fulltext/ED561034.pdf. Retrieved July 2018.

Morgavi, P. 2017. *Chief Reader Report on Student Responses: 2017 AP Italian Language & Culture Free-Response Questions*, College Board. https://secure-media.collegeboard.org/ap/pdf/ap17-chief-reader-report-italian-language.pdf. Retrieved July 2019.

Morgavi, P. 2018. *Chief Reader Report on Student Responses: 2018 AP Italian Language and Culture Free-Response Questions*, College Board. https://apcentral.collegeboard.org/media/pdf/ap18-italian-language-chief-reader-report.pdf. Retrieved July 2019.

Morgavi, P. 2019. *Chief Reader Report on Student Responses: 2019 AP Italian Language and Culture Free-Response Questions*, College Board. https://apcentral.collegeboard.org/media/pdf/ap19-chief-reader-report-italian-language.pdf. Retrieved December 2019.

National Research Center for College and University Admission (NRCCUA). 2008. *2008 ACTFL Student Survey Report*. Lee's Summit (MO): NRCCUA. https://www.actfl.biz/sites/default/files/news/ACTFL_Final_2008_completeLOW.pdf. Retrived July 2019

National Research Center for College and University Admission (NRCCUA). 2010. *2010 Annual Report: Cooperative Research Program*. Lee's Summit (MO): NRCCUA. https://www.actfl.org/sites/default/files/news/NRCCUA%20Cooperative%20Research%20Report%20for%20ACTFL%202010.pdf. Retrieved July 2019.

New York Times. 1940. *War Casts Shadow on School Opening* (September): 25. https://timesmachine.nytimes.com/timesmachine/1940/09/10/113104568.html?pageNumber=25. Retrieved July 2017.

Newman, M. 2011. "Minority Students and A.P. Program, a Mixed Report Card." *The New York Times*, 9 February 2011. https://thechoice.blogs.nytimes.com/2011/02/09/advanced-placement/?rref=collection%2Fbyline%2Fmaria-newman&action=click&contentCollection=undefined&region=stream&module=streamunit&version=latest&contentPlacement=83&pgtype=collection. Retrieved October 2019.

Nuessel, F. 2004. "AP Italian Language and Culture Course and Exam." *Italica* 81.4: 551-557.

Nuessel, F. 2011. "Details on the Reinstated AP Italian Language and Culture." *AATI Newsletter* (Spring): 4-5.

Nuessel, F. 2012. "First AP Italian Language & Culture Exam and First AP Reading in 2006." *AATI Newsletter* (Fall): 8.

Nuessel, F. 2012. *Student Performance Q&A: 2012 AP Italian Language and Culture Free-Response Questions.* https://secure-media.collegeboard.org/apc/ap12_italian_qa.pdf. Retrieved July 2019.

Nuessel, F. 2012. "AP Italian Language and Culture Results 2012." *AATI Newsletter* (Fall): 7.

Nuessel, F. 2012. "Reinstatement of the AP Italian Language and Culture Exam in 2012." *AATI Newsletter* (Fall 2012): 6.

Nuessel, F. 2014. "Message form the President." *AATI Newsletter.* Spring 2014: 1-4.

Pagano, T. 2002. "AATI 2001 General Business Meeting." *Italica* 79.1: 140-144.

Pagano, T. 2004. "AATI 2003 General Business Meeting." *Italica* 81.1: 134-146.

Petrarca Boyle, B., 2016. "National Contest, AP, and College Board." *AATI Newsletter* (Spring 2016): 9.

Romero da Silva, Y. 2017. "History of College Admissions in the U.S." December 2017. *www.nacacnet.org*. October 2019. https://www.nacacnet.org/globalassets/documents/professional-development/guiding-the-way-to-inclusion/2017-presentations/b1history-of-college-admissionyvonneromerodasilva.pdf>. Retrieved July 2019.

Rothschild, E. 1999. "Four Decades of the Advanced Placement Program." *The History Teacher, Special Issue: Advanced Placement,* 32.2: 175-206.

Ryan, C. M. 2016. "Enrollments in Languages other than English." Paper presented at MLA Convention. Austin (TX).

Santini, F., 2021. *Chief Reader Report on Student Responses: 2021 AP Italian Language and Culture Free-Response Questions,* College Board, https://apcentral.collegeboard.org/media/pdf/ap21-chief-reader-report-italian-language.pdf. Retrieved July 2022.

Santini, F. 2022. *Chief Reader Report on Student Responses: 2022 AP Italian Language and Culture Free-Response Questions,* College Board, 2022. https://apcentral.collegeboard.org/media/pdf/ap22-cr-report-italian-language.pdf. Retrieved September 2022.

Sclafani, C. 2004. "AATI 2003 General Business Meeting." *Italica* 81.1: 134-146.

Snouwaert, J. 2020. "Nearly 10,000 students ran into issues submitting their AP exams because of technical glitches." https://www.businessinsider.com/students-experience-issues-submitting-online-ap-exams-2020-5. Retrieved July 2021.

Spolsky, B. 2000. "Language Testing in the Modern Language Journal." *The Modern Language Journal* 84.4: 536- 552.

Stewart, D. M., & Johanek, M. C. 1996. "The Evolution of College Entrance Examinations." https://repository.upenn.edu/cgi/viewcontent.cgi?article=1183&context=gse_pubs. Retrieved July 2109.

Strauss, V. 2020. "College Board says new online AP tests are going well – but students report big problems." https://www.washingtonpost.com/education/2020/05/15/college-board-says-new-online-ap-tests-are-going-well-students-report-big-problems/ Retrieved July 2021.

Striano, A. and Adorno, E. 1969. "United States Colleges and Universities Offering Italian." *Italica* 46.4: 460-472.

Tamburri, A. J. 1991. *To Hyphenate or not to Hyphenate: the Italian/American Writer: Or, An Other American?* Montreal: Guernica Editions.

Tamburri, A. J. 2008. "Messaggio del presidente." *AATI Newsletter* (Spring): 1-4.

Tamburri, A. J. 2009. "Messaggio del presidente." *AATI Newsletter* (Spring): 1-4.

Tamburri, A. J. 2009. "Messaggio del presidente." *AATI Newsletter* (Fall): 1-3.

Thorndike, E. L. and E. G. Thorndike. 1920. "Intelligence Examinations for College Entrance." *The Journal of Educational Research*, 1.5: 329-337.

Turchetta, B. 2005. *Il mondo in Italiano. Varietà ed usi internazionali della lingua*. Bari: Laterza.

Turchetta, B., Vedovelli, M. 2018. *Lo spazio linguistico italiano globale: il caso dell'Ontario*, Pisa: Pacini.

Vedovelli, M. 2014. *Storia linguistica dell'emigrazione italiana nel mondo*, Rome: Carocci.

Vitti-Alexander, M. R. 2010 "AATI General Business Meeting." *Italica* 87.1: 158-163.

Vitti, A. C. 2010. "Messaggio del Presidente." AATI *Newsletter* (Spring): 1.

Vitti, A. C., 2010. "Messaggio del Presidente." AATI *Newsletter* (Fall): 1.

Wall, D. and J.C. Alderson. 1993. "Examining washback: the Sri Lankan Impact Study." *Language Testing* 10.1: 41-69.

Wright, W. E., S. Boun and O. Garcia. 2015. *Handbook of Bilingual and Multilingual Education*. Hoboken, NJ: Wiley & Blackwell.

INDEX

ACIE xiii
ACTFL xi, xiii, xv n11, 21 n19, 55 n13, 56 n14, 56 n26, 59, 60, 64, 66, 70, 77, 91
Adorno, E. xv
Alderson, J.C. 89-90
Angiolillo, P.F. xv, 12
Arcudi, Bruno 12

Bailey, K.M. 90
Baldelli, I. ix
Bancheri, S. 14
Barker, D.G. 1, 20
Barni, M. ix
Bassetti, P. 95
Bettoni xiv
Bigelow, D.N. 20
Boccaccio ix
Boorstein, D.J. 7
Boun, S. 56
Brinsmade, C. 21
Brown H.D. 3
Buchanan, M.A. 1, 21
Butler, K.D. 17

Castiglione, P.B 12
Cavatorta, Beppe 19
Cavatorta, G. xv, 82
Cheng, C. 90, 95
Cordasco, F. x-xi, xv, 10-11
Cosenza, Mario ix-xi, 20, 56
Curtis, A. 95

Dante ix
De Mauro, T. ix
Dolci, R. x-xi, xv

Epstein, M. 15

Falbo, E.S. 12
Flattau, P.E. 7, 20
Freddi ix
Fucilla, J.G. xv, 11
Fuess, C.M. 1, 5, 11

Garica, O. 56

Gifford, B.R. 95
Giordano, P. 15
Giovanardi, C. ix, 39
Golden, H.H. 2, 12-14
Goldberg, D. 56

Haller, H. xv
Hanson, F. 1, 5-6, 20

Jackson, C.A. 20
Jamison, E. 1, 7
Jaschik, S. 34
Johanek, M.C. 20

Klaric, J. 8, 20
Kleinhenz, C 15
Kibler, L. 13

Laggini, J. 12-13, 21
LaGuarida, Fiorello xi
Lanza, I.L. 17
Lawrence, I.M. 20
Lebano, E.A. xv
Liekar, C.Y. 1, 7-8
Looney, D. 56
Lucas, C.J. 1, 7
Lusin, N. 56

Maiellaro, G. 14, 19, 95
Mancini, A. 2
Mattern, K.D. 8, 20
Miraglia, L. ix
Mita, D. 15-16
Mollica, A. 13
Morgan, R. 8, 20
Morgavi, P. 82, 84, 88

Newman, M. 20
Nuessel, F. 16, 82

O'Connor, M.C. 95

Pagano, T. 15-19
Petrarca, B. ix, 21
Prezzolini, Giuseppe xi
Pope, Denise 8, 20

Rigol, G. 20
Romer da Silva, Y. 5
Rothschild, E. 7, 8, 20
Ryan, C. xv

Santini, F. 82, 84-85, 87-88
Sclafani, C. 16
Show, E.J. 8
Snouwaret, J. 34
Spolsky, B. 21
Stewart, D.M. 20
Strauss, V. 34
Striano, A. xv

Tamburri, A.J. xv, 16-17, 21, 56
Thorndike, E.G. 6, 20
Thorndike, E.L. 6, 20
Trifone, P. ix, 39
Turchetta, B. xiv

Van Essen, T. 20
Vedovelli, T. ix
Vitti-Alexander, M.R. 14, 21

Wall, D. 89
Watanbe, Y. 90, 95
Wright, W.E. 56

Xiong, X 8, 20

Author

ROBERTO DOLCI is Associate Professor of Educational Linguistics at the University for Foreigners in Perugia. He is also visiting Scholar at the John D. Calandra Italian American Institute (Queens College, CUNY). His main research interests are plurilingualism, pluriculturalism, and language policies. He is co-editor of the journal TILCA (*Teaching Italian Language and Culture Annual*). He has written extensively on Educational Linguistics and Teacher Education. With Anthony Julian Tamburri he has co-edited *Why Study Italian: Diverse Perspectives on a Theme* (John D. Calandra Italian American Institute, 2013), and *Intercomprehension and Plurilingualism. Assets for Italian Language in the USA* (John D. Calandra Italian American Institute, 2015). He is the author of *Il Giornalino di Prezzolini. La lingua Italiana tra promozione e propaganda nella New York degli anni '30 e '40* (Franco Cesati Editore, 2018).

www.ingramcontent.com/pod-product-compliance
Lightning Source LLC
Chambersburg PA
CBHW080604170426
43196CB00017B/2902